CPAC

Doris Day

The illustrated
biography

Doris Day

The illustrated biography

Michael Freedland

ANDRE
DEUTSCH

FOR:
Beryl and Paul
Helen and Maurice
Maureen and Vivian
Rachel and Harold
In beloved friendship.

First published in 2000 by
André Deutsch
an imprint of the
Carlton Publishing Group
20 Mortimer Street
London W1T 3JW

Reprinted in 2008

A CIP catalogue record for this book is available from the
British Library

ISBN 978 0 233 00262 0

PHOTOGRAPHS REPRODUCED BY PERMISSION OF:
The Kobal Collection (pages 66, 111 & 117);
The Movie Store Collection (pages 41, 58, 113 & 114);
Corbis Images Ltd (page 123); Pictorial Press (all other pages)

Printed and bound in Dubai

CONTENTS

A Sentimental Journey

She was never an ordinary singer, Doris Day. Never one of those chanteuses who stood in front of a band and sang her heart out – and every other inch of her body, too. She wasn't one of those who needed to wipe the sweat off her brow before every encore. Neither was she one of those simpering vocalists who seemed to lull an unsuspecting male into believing she had fallen in love with him.

No. Doris Day sang a song as though she meant it – but also with the firm knowledge that that was what people wanted to hear. There were quiet ballads and there were louder, more raucous ones. Unlike so many others of her calling, she knew how to adapt her style to each. When she sang 'The Deadwood Stage', you knew that there was a whip somewhere handy (a phrase that would have a great deal more meaning in these less inhibited days, a different association entirely from the one that she would have recognized as Calamity Jane, in an age when calamity meant an addiction to the Coke that came in a bottle, not sniffed up the nose). But when she sang that, there was a tickle in her voice and, whether you could see her or not, you knew those pearly white teeth were locked in the middle of a smile.

She only had to say 'Que Sera Sera' and audiences on five continents would immediately, and in unison, offer the translation 'What Will Be, Will Be'. And then there was 'Ten Cents a Dance': you didn't cry when you heard that – because you knew that she wasn't pretending to cry either. It was a song and she sang it as a song – no more.

There are, of course, people who would complain about that.

And about her movies, too – for it was the cinema that saw Doris Day at her best. It was her films that got her the biggest audiences. Looking back now, more than thirty years since her last movie left the cinema circuits, not even they are always remembered the way they should be – as entertainment, pure and simple, for an age when people didn't want unnecessary complications interfering with their enjoyment.

The organizers of a Doris Day festival at London's National Film Theatre in 1980 put it all too bluntly. To some, they said, Doris had 'come to epitomize the unacceptable face of the 1950s and 1960s to the post-1968 generation. She is associated with a repressive or at least normative, sexuality. She is the model of 1950s and early 1960s maidenhood before marriage and heterosexual monogamy afterwards – in short the cornerstone of the nuclear family.'

Oh dear. But Doris Day wouldn't have recognized any such philosophical summaries. That wasn't the kind of trade she was in.

She did, however, once say: 'I was never a feminist. I was punchy, but never hard. Remember that my career women were always single, and I played my fair share of moms at home, too.' Not at the same time, it has to be said.

And, in the best of them, she always had a song to go with the title and that was what the folks came to see. On records, she sang songs for people to listen to, in the days when those people used to sit snugly in front of a roaring fire as they put either the old, black breakable 78 discs on their record player or started experimenting with those funny little seven-inch things the trade knew as 45s.

It was a time when they played request discs on radio programmes and, if you chose your show carefully, you knew when a Doris Day record was likely to be aired. Right back to when she first sang 'It's Magic', people listened to her renditions on picnics and at garden parties – because hers was the voice that not only tickled, but soothed at the same time.

Lyricists liked her because she always enunciated their words perfectly. In truth, however, people liked Doris Day's singing without ever really listening to those words. There was a voice out there that was pure velvet and you heard it much as you heard a sweet trumpet player, not for dramatic effect. It was a musical experience and you didn't actually need to know the words to enjoy it, any more than you had to accept some fanciful explanation of the real 'meaning' behind a composer's symphony before you could appreciate it. You sat listening to those old Doris Day records simply because you enjoyed the sound they made, not the story they supposedly told.

She was the living embodiment of the roles she played in all those old Warner Bros musicals. She was, after all, the one who would be handed a brand new sheet of music, hot off the gnarled fingers of the man who had just sat down at the upright piano keyboard, and immediately sing it as though it had been taught to her by the music teacher at good old Hollywood High. She did it in film after film. Danny Thomas showed her the words and music he had just miraculously dreamed up in – what else – *I'll See You in My Dreams* and she performed it the way she had no doubt rehearsed it a dozen times before the cameras started turning. Wistfully, she repeated the feat in

Doris and youthful fans in the 1950s

Young at Heart in which a down-trodden, the world-owes-me-a-living type of guy played by Frank Sinatra created a masterpiece just to be recited by our Doris.

That was always faintly ridiculous – as ridiculous as those wide, long, deep street scenes that somehow appeared on the stages of theatres in the early Busby Berkeley movies. Yes, we may have sniggered a bit. But it didn't really matter. Doris Day films were usually fast, even when they weren't funny, and you didn't have to waste time with explanations. All that mattered was that Doris sang and after she had finished

Doris Day

singing, you walked out of a theatre whistling the number – not the name of the last person on an everlasting list of credits.

Yes, it was a simpler age when our Doris starred in all those films. You can't forget them easily because they usually – *Calamity Jane* was the exception – fitted into one of two categories (and if they didn't, you plainly would forget them). In her very earliest days, she was the one with that porcelain smile, the long blonde hair and the swinging dirndl skirt, richly patterned to take care of that much-sought-after rarity, Technicolor. Or, in her later movies, she was the one that the dress designers loved. Her hair was shorter now, but they enjoyed giving her little hats to wear, ones that matched the coats that didn't add a degree of warmth to her body. But, you always told yourself, she was such a warm person, she didn't need them.

Hollywood, however, had always had a love affair with her, just as it always worshipped Christmas – and Doris Day was never allowed to escape the festive season either. So, when she wasn't too busy decorating the tree, she was usually ready for the scene by the front door when she kissed the children goodnight while adjusting the full-length sable coat (with matching hat, natch) that she would afterwards hate herself for ever wearing.

To generations of film-goers, those clothes were as important as the songs – and, it is true to say, the stories were as inconsequential as the lyrics. People, young and not quite so young, would sit contentedly in their seats and let the tales waft over them. It was because everything looked so good, the songs sounded so nice and Doris was, well, so nice, too.

You usually knew what was going to happen, particularly in those movies with Rock Hudson. He hated her, she pined after him, he mistook her intentions and she didn't like what was going on, he found out the truth and now she was standing no nonsense. You knew it was all going to work out fine in the end. The only point at issue was how. People always paid their money and were content to let the studios make their choice. Meanwhile, you inevitably knew that Doris would be pleased with that choice because she always did it so well. Only later on would we discover that she frequently wasn't pleased at all.

She would never claim to have been one of the cinema's finest actresses, but those films were cut for her as artfully as were her outfits.

And the songs were always just right. I've never heard anyone complain about the songs she sang. There just was nothing to complain about. She was as made-to-measure for her age – and that of those of us who remember seeing those films the first time around, when we had to pay for the privilege – as were her songs and her clothes. We liked it like that and she knew that we did because the studios kept asking for more.

Doris Day arrived in our lives before the advent of rock'n'roll, punk and the more contemporary meaning of boogie. She would never have fitted into an age when girl singers dyed their hair – not just blonde, but that scary shade of blood-red – and pierced their noses with safety pins. You knew Doris Day had never seen a safety pin in her life. She was always far too refined for that.

It was like those film stories again. In her movies, you just knew that both she and the man in her life would never do more than merely kiss – and be extremely content for ever after. If she had children, you knew for a fact that all those medical books and how-to sex manuals had got it wrong. In her case, no, she didn't want any nonsense about having them delivered by storks. That was quite ridiculous. No, they had to have come from underneath somebody's gooseberry bush, although probably not hers. When, in those far-off days, did you ever see a pregnant woman who looked pregnant?

But, it must now be said, as far as she was concerned, it wasn't always like that. As the wag Oscar Levant famously put it, he remembered Doris Day from the time before she became a virgin. In fact, that is what makes her story so fascinating.

It is also why, when she made *Love Me or Leave Me*, the shock of seeing her being beaten up by the vicious Marty the Gimp (James Cagney to you) was so palpable. Our Doris? Grown men wrote in anger to MGM, protesting. There were others, I am sure, who wanted to march up to the screen and give Mr Cagney a punch in the kisser.

When she made the heart-breaking *Midnight Lace*, it wasn't what audiences wanted of her. They craved for songs, not the story – even though Ms Day looked as elegant as ever.

Yes, that was the word. Elegant. In my earliest days as a journalist, I ran a film column for a local newspaper. Only a raw beginner would dare do what I did when I rang up a studio press office for stills of Doris Day. 'I'd particularly like some cheesecake,' I said.

It would have been kinder if the man at the other end had merely directed me to the nearest bakery. Instead, he protested: 'Miss Day' (it was, after all, a long time ago, a time before ladies liked to be addressed as 'Ms') 'does not do cheesecake.' No, of course she didn't. She would have been a totally different person if she had, and we wouldn't have liked her nearly as much.

Neither did she do many of the things people expected of film stars. She wasn't often seen at film premières, she didn't do much in the way of commercial sponsorship – that wouldn't have been nice either – and she plainly hated publicity unless it was absolutely necessary. Live appearances? Forget them.

She didn't do much, either, in the way of going round the world entertaining troops. The war was over by the time she hit the top and she was badly needed at home.

No, she knew her place. And that place was always on a movie screen or spinning around a record turntable, the kind you could see, not locked away on what one

With James Cagney in *Love Me or Leave Me*

Doris Day

broadcaster likes to call a 'shaving mirror' in some electronic drawer.

Yet none of these things are criticisms of her. On the contrary, they are tributes to a facility that many another star would bitterly envy – providing audiences around the world with what they wanted and what they expected. What she had was a staying power that few of the women (or men, for that matter) singers who came after her would ever boast.

When *Calamity Jane* or *Love Me or Leave Me* is on a television screen, it never serves as one of those movies that provides time-filling material. TV companies are never able to buy a Doris Day film as part of some package deal or other. They know that when those lips form around those teeth and sing an old favourite, the ratings are going to go up. They have to go up – because they always *have* gone up. That is truly an enviable reputation for any star to have.

And that is precisely what you have to call her – a star. A STAR in capital letters, not because of some indefinable quality – we have already defined it – but because people have always wanted to see and hear her the way they always had seen and heard her.

Yet, to be fair to her and to us, there were limitations. She was never one of those stars of whom you could say, 'Even when she was not particularly good, you knew you were in the presence of greatness.' She was never a Judy Garland, whose brilliant moments always excused the dreadful performances that littered her later years. Neither was she like, say, Al Jolson, who had his detractors but stunned even them with the electrifying, almost nuclear, quality of his stage performances. Doris Day was always good, always reliable, always, in her way, exciting – and that was what made her a star.

It would be easy to say that the idea of this book is simply to tell a story because of that fame and that reputation. She deserves much more than that.

Unlike a great many entertainers, and like those films, her own story isn't merely bland and insignificant. If it had been, offering you these next pages would be to cheat. The Doris Day story is the mirror opposite of those movie scripts and those song lyrics. For once, don't simply think of the pictures as the real 'music' and not bother with the words.

That is perhaps not a surprising admonition from a writer. Of course, he wants his words to be read. But in this case, the words are important simply because the tale they tell is important. Doris Day wasn't always a success. Nor has she escaped the problems of this life. She is not alone among the Hollywood community in failing to find happiness in her life. The perpetual screen virgin married four times – never leaving either the divorce court or the funeral parlour less than angry as well as sad. How that happened, this book will try to explain.

But why in this format? Because Doris Day has always been in a category all of her own and because so much of what she has done has been so visual, this seemed to both my publishers and me to be the way to tell that story – to tell and to explain and to illustrate, but not to get bogged down in the kind of detail that doesn't lend itself to this particular subject.

It is not one of those biographies that wants to spellbind by words that become more the focus of attention than the details of the life they are supposed to describe. Nor is it going to want to put the subject on some kind of printed psychiatrist's couch. (The very notion of putting Doris Day on a couch would be far too unseemly in any case. It would impolite and I don't intend to be that.) But, while it won't attempt a *National Enquirer* kind of exposé, neither is it going to escape those unhappy moments that those old fan magazines like *Photoplay* or *Picturegoer* would eschew so vehemently.

And it will ask the occasional question – not merely why did she stop entertaining the way she used to do, but more, did she have to do so? Was it just advancing years or did she get fed up with the business? Is there not, for instance, just a tinge of eccentricity in her devotion to lost pets?

How much of her life was the result of the events that shaped it? Did she work as hard at controlling that life as she plainly did in the work that she performed not just so well, but so diligently?

In short, was it work that drove her on, or was it simply following the maxim of *que sera, sera*?

My Dream is Yours

Cincinnati is as good a place as any to begin, if you are going to start life in show business. It's the sort of town a star might be proud to say she hailed from but is very pleased to have left.

These days, its showbiz connections are fairly limited – to the extent of the extremely large and curvy towers of the Procter and Gamble building being referred to as 'Dolly Parton'. Ms Parton came a long time after Doris Day's heyday and was a different kind of singer altogether. When Doris was born, on 3 April 1924, fashion decreed that the kind of attributes that would make Dolly so famous – her breasts, not her bravura performances – were strictly passé and were there to be hidden. Cincinnati, however, encouraged people to go out and perform to their heart's content. Not just Ms Day, but also the Mills Brothers, and a handful of others who made it big after starting out in the Ohio city.

But you'd have to be pretty prescient to forecast that this child would ever have her name in lights – at least from the evidence of her first public stage performance.

It was the one at kindergarten that made a little embarrassed girl called Doris Kappelhoff go running off the stage. She was playing in the olio – the chorus warm-up to the main performance – of a minstrel show in the age when such things were not just forgivable, but quaint and expected.

These were not the sort of routines that made Al Jolson's name – the kind in which the black servant always got the best of the wicked plantation owner and earned the gratitude of black performers who were themselves banned from big-time vaudeville.

Doris, to her later distaste, had to recite lines that included words like 'niggie'. But that was not her only shame.

She blacked up her face and she also blacked the red panties that her mother had sewn to her dress, sewn them so well that she wasn't able to get them off in time to avoid wetting herself. The audience roared with laughter and Doris Kappelhoff ran off, totally humiliated. To that one incident goes the dubious credit for Doris Day's reluctance to appear before a live audience.

Not that she ever thought about such things in those days. She certainly never thought about her later image as the girl who did everything so properly. When old enough for matters of that sort to mean anything at all, she was already carrying the kind of baggage unknown at the height of the Doris Day movie career. She had had the experience of her parents' broken marriage – again in circumstances that a well-bred (even a badly bred) child should never have known about.

It was at a party at her Cincinnati home that, while pretending to be asleep, she saw her father going into a bedroom with a woman who wasn't her mother. She not only saw him, she would relate in her autobiography, she heard him and she heard the woman. She heard things that one would think no child would ever begin to understand. Doris cried herself to sleep that night. Later, she was taken by her mother to wait outside a house in another part of the city – where they saw her father go inside with the woman she had watched and heard so painfully at the party.

That wasn't the only problem in the household. William and Alma Kappelhoff quarrelled even when there wasn't another woman on the scene. They argued about money, always about money. They also quarrelled over the future of their children, Doris and Paul.

Her father, a music teacher who liked to be known as 'The Professor', wanted Doris to follow in his footsteps. He was sure that she would make an excellent concert pianist. Alma saw music in her future, too, although only the kind that she would be able to dance to.

But the idea of Mr Kappelhoff sleeping with another woman and enjoying things with her that he never could with his wife – that decided matters once and for all.

He left home soon afterwards and Doris slept with her mother that night.

Of German parentage, William Kappelhoff was a man who matched most of the stereotypes of the large German colony that had established itself in Cincinnati. He was, on the surface, a pedantic, terribly proper man. He was organist at the local Catholic church and ran a choral group there that was the envy of all the other music teachers in Cincinnati.

He was also racially intolerant, hated blacks, who were 'niggers'(ironical, bearing in mind that in old age he married a black woman) and Jews, who were 'kikes'. As I say, he was the stereotype. There were any number of Germans in Cincinnati who were not racists and, indeed, the city was the seat of one of American Reform Jewry's principal theological establishments, the Hebrew Union College. Had Herr Professor Kappelhoff known of its existence, he would doubtless have picketed the building.

Doris would later admit that she accepted everything he said. She knew no Jews, no blacks (real blacks, that is, not the ones who were mocked in the minstrel show) and, until that night at the party, accepted that Daddy had to be right.

Whether her mother accepted it, too, is a matter of doubt. Mrs Alma Kappelhoff was the mirror image of her husband. She also came from German stock – her parents were born in Berlin – and might have been considered to have the sort of ideas that, stereotypes again, were thought to have come from that background. But she didn't. She was a fun-loving woman who would approve totally of her daughter's entry into the world of singing and acting for a living. After all, she named her daughter after her favourite film star, Doris Kenyon (who would later become a Beverly Hills neighbour of the now much more famous Doris). Doris was her third child. In addition to her older brother Paul, there had been one still older who had died before Doris was born.

It was Alma's idea that Doris should go to a dancing school. After all, the Herr Professor was no longer around, nor were his ambitions for his daughter becoming a concert pianist. He had particularly hated the idea of her taking dancing lessons: by ensuring that Doris did go to dancing school, Alma was doubtless – even if only psychologically – getting some kind of satisfaction from the effect it would have on her errant spouse. Revenge was about the only thing that was sweet in her life.

Nevertheless, whichever way you looked at it, going to dancing classes seemed to be an inspired idea. Doris was good at dancing, so good that everyone who saw her suggested she should take it up professionally. But, even if she decided that she never would do that, it was a good school and going there made her happy.

There she met a twelve-year-old boy called Jerry Docherty. It was probably Alma who had the idea that her little girl and young Master Docherty should team up and perform as what show people called a double act – playing for masonic evenings and other private functions at which the local gentry were not allowed to see the kind of girls they would really have wanted to spend their money on viewing.

But the kids were good – better than Doris herself really believed. They went in for a competition, sang and danced their hearts out for heat after heat, week after week. They won every one of them. They also won the championship – and $500 along with it.

By now Mrs Kappelhoff had become what tradition has come to call a stage mother. Docherty's mother had too, and between them they cooked up the idea that it would be reasonable to take their two talented children off to Hollywood.

It wasn't that they had any idea of putting them through the movies, but in the 1930s – as now – Hollywood was the centre not just of the film industry, the one that actually made motion pictures, but of all the ancillary businesses, too. The two women believed it was there that their children would get proper training from a proper instructor, the kind who was used to seeing his protégés dancing on screens all over the world.

Doris in 1936, at the age of twelve

The mothers chose a man who had himself danced in the movies – contrary to the adage that those who can, do, those who can't, teach. The improbably named Louis de Pron did both. He taught the children to dance as though it was as natural as walking. Unfortunately, it wasn't. Nor was walking, as Doris soon discovered.

It was in 1937, when Doris was thirteen, that Mrs Kappelhoff took her back to Cincinnati, ostensibly just for a short stay. California was now where she wanted to make her home and, in Alma's mind, it was a done deal.

She had to go home to make the final arrangements for renting out her apartment. While there, she gladly accepted the idea of some close friends giving her and her children an official send-off party at their home at Hamilton, near Cincinnati. It was a Friday in October – Friday, 13 October 1937. It wasn't easy to keep a thirteen-year-old at a boring adult party, and when some older friends suggested they take off for a hamburger at a local eaterie, Doris was more than happy to accept.

She couldn't have known that that trip would mark the end of her dancing days and the beginning of her career as a singer. There was also a tune that would have considerable impact on her life.

The Winning Team

T he price of that hamburger would turn out to be higher than anyone could have expected. The cost wasn't just to be reckoned in money, but in the effect it would have on her life.

Doris and her three friends drove to the hamburger joint, stayed just a short time, and then drove back again. The young man driving the car – it had probably seen much better days and the youngster's driving skills were probably no more to be recommended – was full of the joy of youth and so was his girlfriend. So full that they lost their way and didn't realize when they approached the railway level crossing that they were about to crash into a passing freight train.

The driver and the three other passengers were thrown through the shattered windscreen. Thirteen-year-old Doris crawled out of the wreckage and couldn't feel her right leg. She fainted and woke up in hospital to be told that it had been severely fractured.

Just how severely broken it really was was kept from her. So was the fact that she would probably never dance again. For eighteen months she hobbled around with the aid of crutches, the leg encased in a plaster cast that did little for her morale and nothing at all for her dancing.

That was how she spent her fifteenth birthday. Moping about her condition – and listening to records by a wonderful young black singer who had had a big hit about a girl who sang of her 'little yellow basket' that rhymed with 'A Tisket, a Tasket'. (The young singer was of course Ella Fitzgerald.)

Hearing that was a brief hiatus from all the pain she was suffering – which became compounded when a Manchester terrier called Tiny was run over and died in her arms. She would remember that moment for ever afterwards.

Only the music made her feel better, it seemed. One day, listening to that radio, she

Doris and her mother Alma in 1960, on the *Midnight Lace* set

thought she would get the better of her condition. She threw the crutches away and decided to dance. Tried to dance, more truthfully. Failed to dance, in fact. The song was 'Tea for Two', but the next cup of tea was strictly for one – and in a hospital room.

She had fallen down with the kind of thud she had last heard when the car plunged into the freight train. All the good the months in the cast had done was instantly undone. Worse, there were more breaks. It took a year for the fractures finally to heal.

What didn't heal was the idea of her never dancing again.

It was here that having a mother like Alma Kappelhoff really came into its own. Doris has always insisted that Alma was not like other stage mothers, the kind who pushed their kids forward in directions they had no wish to go – but convinced them that it was not only for their own good and where they had wanted to travel to all along.

No, by all accounts, Mrs Kappelhoff was a good psychologist, understood her child's needs and tried to direct them the way she thought her Doris might like. She also based that view on some extensive research – like casually hearing the girl sing along with whatever band was playing at the time. It was then that she had the idea that Doris might become a singer, a better singer than she could ever have been a dancer. History records this as one of the most sensible decisions that this German *hausfrau* ever made.

Doris Day

The fan magazines recording the success of the young Doris Day a decade or so later would enthuse that the blonde actress had always believed that everything was for the best and just calmly looked forward to a future that was different, but no less exciting, than the one she had left behind. It would be nice to think that she thought it a thoroughly wonderful thing that she had broken her leg in more places than was quite decent. It is highly unlikely that she simply whispered '*Que sera sera*' to herself (twenty years before she ever thought of singing those words) and got down to that new career her mother was earmarking for her.

But Alma, with Doris's co-operation, found out about a singing teacher named Grace Raine. Ms Raine, in turn, introduced her to Andrew Carlin, who ran an amateur talent programme called 'Carlin's Carnival' on the Cincinnati local radio station, WLW. He heard Doris Kappelhoff sing a number called 'Day After Day' and thought that the girl on the crutches could have something.

He got her to sing 'Day After Day' week after week – on the Saturday morning show. She, of course, didn't get paid. WLW was hitherto best known for its programme featuring Frank Simon and the Armco Band (sponsored by the local steel works) which specialized in the music of John Philip Sousa. It would have one other claim to fame. It was there that the Mills Brothers made their début.

As in all the best show biz stories, Doris was noticed. Not in a big way, but people heard her singing on the 'Carnival' programme and asked to hear more. And not just on the programme. Charlie Yee, the proprietor of a local Chinese restaurant, the Shanghai Inn, heard her, too, and once a week the young teenager performed there – not just quiet and smooth songs like 'Day After Day' which one might think suited the persona of the singer we have come to know and love, but raucous numbers like 'Murder She Said', which would soon become the Betty Hutton standard.

Doris, for her part, wasn't beyond contemplating murdering some members of the Shanghai Inn's clientele. It was unnerving having to sing over the din of cutlery being rattled and china being taken on and off tables, to say nothing of the seemingly rude and insensitive continuing conversation. Like the time she wet her pants in the juvenile minstrel show, it didn't exactly point her in the direction of a live stage career as her ultimate goal. But it did get her started in what would be, in a remarkably short time, an amazing career.

There were, naturally enough, several steps on the way – and several people to direct those steps.

The first of these people was the local bandleader Barney Rapp. She told Rapp that she was eighteen, a nice age to be invited to join his band – which she was ready to do. It would be for no more than a try out, but in her mind, it was joining his band, and that was good enough to get on with.

She didn't know that at least 100 other girls had had similar aspirations. But Doris Kappelhoff was the one he chose. At The Sign of the Drum, a restaurant just outside Cincinnati, the sixteen-year-old made her professional début, singing 'A Foggy Day', the Gershwin number that both Fred Astaire and Frank Sinatra took as their own.

Doris would say that she remembered very little about that number, but Barney Rapp did and so did the diners and dancers at The Sign of the Drum. Rapp knew from listening to that one song that he had made the right choice. She was on her way to somewhere big and Rapp wanted to be on the journey with her.

She sang for him for six nights a week. He was so struck by her talent and the reaction it brought from his customers that he decided that she ought to have billing. The only trouble was – and this is probably the most often-told story in all those Hollywood how-they-made-it musicals – he didn't think the name sounded very good – and it looked even worse on the marquee outside the restaurant. It had to go. But to what?

'How about La Ponselle,' he suggested, although why can only be guessed at. One guess might be that the Ponselle sisters were eminent opera singers a generation before Doris was even thought of. Although how that would fit in with the sort of music that Rapp was playing takes some figuring out. He also suggested 'Marmaduke' – which had even less reason behind it. 'Doris Kapp?' well, that might not be a bad idea. It would certainly fit in logically with a girl born Doris Kappelhoff. Rapp could then have reasoned that Jack Kapp was the name of the head of Decca Records, and giving Doris the same name might seem like an attempt at nepotism that was sure to backfire – Kapp would never employ her himself and none of the opposition labels would either, for precisely the same reason.

And then he thought about the first song he had heard her sing on the radio, and the one that had become something of a mascot for her at the restaurant, the one she sang so much, 'Day After Day'.

'We'll call you "Doris Day",' he said. She didn't like it. 'It sounded really cheap,' she would say years later. 'Like a burlesque singer. "Doris Day and her Dove Dance", that sort of thing.'

But he was the boss and she was only sixteen. Mr Rapp probably didn't know that there was already an actress by the same name making B westerns for Republic studios. Even if he had, it wouldn't have mattered. Doris was going to be a band singer, not a film actress. And certainly not one who made movies like *Saga of Death Valley*.

So Doris Day she became. And that's how it all started.

28

Starlift

T here were a number of new events on what was now the Doris Day horizon. And new people, too. If Barney Rapp had been her career salvation, he was now, indirectly, also on the way to having a profound influence on her private life. It was all due to the people he chose to sit in his band – particularly a young trombonist called Al Jorden.

Jorden was ready to release Rapp from one of his less specific responsibilities – as Doris's unofficial guardian and chaperone. He was now the one who drove her home at night and sat with her while they were both were waiting to go on stage. Before long, Doris and Jorden were more than just unofficial guardian and ward. They began dating, not as seriously in her eyes as in his – or in those of his mother, a woman who believed that the young singer was making serious inroads into territory that was very much her own.

Meanwhile, Doris tried to disabuse her of any such worries. She informed the older woman that she had no plans in that direction, but the musician's mother was not convinced.

However, the young man did have romantic intentions and Doris didn't seem to object. When Jorden took a job with the Gene Krupa band, they wrote to each other – letters that apparently got more and more intimate. By the time that, before very long, he left Krupa to join the much better known Jimmy Dorsey band, their relationship-by-correspondence was heating up considerably.

Doris Day was just a teenager and apparently didn't realize what she was getting into. But then she was working so hard now that anything as flattering and tempting as a romance, even one by proxy, was a wonderful diversion. Besides which, her own mother encouraged the relationship – perhaps more than she should have done. Maybe it was because her own romantic life had been so disastrous.

One thing was sure – love was indeed that diversion from hard work. Barney Rapp had closed the Drum and was taking his band on the road, as a freelance operator. That meant that Doris, along with his other musicians, spent the early evening and then the early hours of the next day on a bus going from one gig to another. In dance halls all over her part of the country, they played and she sang all the songs of the day, contemporary hits like 'That Old Black Magic' and soulful jazz pieces like 'St Louis Blues'.

She was young and could take a routine that would have exhausted anyone older – and not a few of her own contemporaries. It wasn't doing her much good either – as she still hobbled on to a bandstand, swapping her walking stick for the stand-up microphone.

That was why a call from Grace Raine proved so enticing. She had heard that Bob Crosby – Bing's youngest brother – was looking for a singer for his highly successful band, the Bobcats. It would mean less running around, let alone more money and more prestige. The bandleader heard her, liked what he heard and, the next night, introduced the charming young Doris Day as his new discovery, the new girl singer with Bob Crosby and the Bobcats.

Crosby operated out of Chicago and Doris and her mother packed up their home in Cincinnati, but this was a Big Band in the Big Band age and, just as Mr Rapp had been, the Bobcats were constantly on the move. And when they were, Doris went with them – although, much to her chagrin, Alma had to stay behind.

Doris loved it. At first. She was very popular, not just with Al on those rare occasions when she saw him, but with the men in the band and those who saw her perform. She was pretty, had a little pert way of standing and, it is said, had the kind of breasts that made them drool.

Not at all the image that Hollywood was to create for her. This was in the time before Doris Day became a virgin.

Before long, she and Al Jorden were married. Now she was having the opportunity she had always wanted – to prove to her mother that a marriage could be happy.

But not hers. She would later say that on her wedding day, she realized it had all been a mistake. He was, she said, a Jekyll and Hyde character with a sadistic streak. He was violent from the moment they were first alone together as man and wife in a bedroom. On that first day of their marriage, he struck her so violently she fell down.

Their first fights – totally one-sided: this was, after all, a completely mystified seventeen-year-old – had been over the very body that made her bandleaders so proud of her, the hips and bust that really did excite men who came to see the band at work. Jorden thought those assets were reason to consider his child wife a whore. Doris may have known who had hit her, but not what. When she became pregnant, quite early on, he demanded that she have an abortion. She adamantly refused. He hit her again – and again. On one occasion, he pointed a gun at Doris's belly – letting her know, in no uncertain terms, that he wanted both his wife and his unborn child dead before either of them had any idea what life was all about.

Another time she told him to slow down while he was driving uncontrollably fast. She said that he was about to kill them both. He said that was precisely what he had in mind. Miraculously, the baby survived all this. Doris called her new son Terry.

A year later, eighteen-year-old Doris Day was divorced. Terry stayed with his mother. Later, he moved in with his mother's mother – and before long he would cease to be Terry Jorden.

Doris's days with the Bobcats were over before she had her baby. Bob Crosby already had one girl singer and couldn't afford the expense of transporting two young women from one engagement to another. Whether the ladies had already started scratching each other's eyes out is not on the record.

Alma continued to look after the baby while Doris looked for new work. But it wasn't easy – either the idea of working or simply getting over the pregnancy. Alma, however, was sufficiently prescient to know what would happen if she allowed her daughter to fall into the trap of becoming just the sort of hausfrau she herself had turned into.

It was Alma's idea that Doris go back to radio station WLW, which no longer had either Frank Simon's Armco band or the Mills Brothers. She did. She sang for the station owner, who took her on – but with little hope of great financial reward. As he said, she had to have a sponsor and without one, she would be merely filling in time.

Thousands of others in the radio business had been given such an injunction and thousands of others had seen careers flounder because they hadn't been able to manage that fateful opportunity.

But Doris's time appears to have been worth spending. She was heard by a scout from MGM who immediately agreed to sponsor a regular fifteen-minute programme – one that was advertising forthcoming attractions from the studio which was already justifying letters that now seemed to stand for Makers of Great Musicals.

The programme proved extraordinarily popular. So popular, in fact, that once more Alma was the one with the big idea. In that area of the country, she told her daughter, WLW was an important station that everyone, in those pre-television days, liked to listen to. But it was just for that neck of the American woods. There was a whole lot of country that had never heard of either WLW or a blonde singer called Doris Day.

She had to think of something permanent.

And she was good enough to get a new job. She had done some work with Fred

Waring and His Pennsylvanians, but there was no security there. Mr Waring had no room for another permanent singer. So she was, as they say, at liberty.

But help was at hand. In the band world, everybody knew what everybody else was doing, without having to be given the information in the pages of *Billboard* or any of the other trade papers.

Les Brown, later to accompany Frank Sinatra and be musical director of practically everything that Bob Hope ever did on television and on stage, heard about her and offered the young Doris Day a job which she accepted more than merely willingly: she was ecstatic to get it. An eighteen-year-old was too young to stay at home and look after a baby and both she and Alma realized it.

Les Brown, for his part, realized that they were made for each other, too – particularly after their first engagement together at the Chicago Theatre Café owned by Mike Todd – later to be the developer of the Todd AO film process and producer-husband of Elizabeth Taylor. The headliner for those early 1940 gigs was the woman known as the world's greatest stripper, Gypsy Rose Lee. Doris and the band performed for dancing for two twenty-five-minute segments.

She began at the rate of $75 a week. By the time she sang with Les Brown and His Band of Renown at one-night stands in New York City, Doris was earning up to $200 a week, colossal money for anyone in those pre-Pearl Harbor days. 'Oh, she was worth it,' Les Brown told me when discussing those times. 'She was very unusual and people liked her.'

For her part, Doris was to describe the bandleader as a father figure, although he himself was still only in his twenties.

What his audiences seemed to like about Doris were those very girl-next-door looks that at the time she would have been grateful to shake off. She no doubt accepted Louis B. Mayer's dictum that if you wanted the girl next door, you knocked on the door next door to find her. But this young mother was grateful to be wanted.

When she began recording with the band, Les noticed that this girl who had always considered herself a Northerner had a distinct Southern pronunciation. The proximity of Cincinnati to Kentucky had obviously had its effect.

For the moment, that was her style and no one complained.

Les Brown didn't exactly say 'stay with me, honey and I'll see you right', but the message was clear enough.

In those days, Brown, the father figure, always seemed to be around when he was needed – and a father was precisely what Doris required most. She might have had a baby of her own, but in many people's eyes – not least in those of the government – she was still a child.

That was a good enough reason for the bandleader to cherish her. To him she was the mainstay of the Band of Renown. He knew that that renown was even more pronounced with Doris up front with him.

But that didn't mean that she enjoyed it. Butterflies before a performance were a serious problem. Before every show, she would, she said, retreat to the nearest toilet 'with one end or the other erupting'.

But somehow even bodily functions couldn't influence Doris's addiction to her business. She didn't merely go with Les and his men on those sometimes painful one-night stands, travelling in the band bus in all weathers, she recorded with him, too. The title of one song seemed singularly appropriate for all those trips. But it was more than just a title. It was a beautiful melody and she sang it with all the heart it required to match the tune with a superbly lyrical performance. It also proved to be an important step on what even then looked like a road to stardom. The song was called 'Sentimental Journey'.

The Thrill of It All

It is perhaps difficult today to really imagine what the Big Bands were and what they represented. These days, they are spoken of in much the same way as silent movies – a fascinating constituent of a time when entertainment was simpler, less demanding, and when people had fun doing things that no one would want to do now.

It is now worth asking whether Doris Day would have made it sixty years later, at a time when the word 'band' frequently means either four singing girls without voices or a gang of three or four dirty-looking youngsters who make millions from shouting as loud as they can into a poor inoffensive microphone. They chant (you couldn't call it singing) a 'lyric' that they have written themselves, which is perhaps five or six words long and which usually forms the title of the piece as well. However, since no one can even hear what those words are, any complaint about not hearing the lyric becomes totally superfluous.

So the answer is, no, Doris Day would not have made it sixty years later. At least, not singing the way she sang 'Sentimental Journey'. This was a blues singer and that southern accent was inescapable. In less than a decade the girl with whom the world fell in love (the one whose voice now seems to have transcended the years) would sound very different indeed.

There doesn't seem to be any way in which her career would have taken the same shape. Had she had that accident in 1997 instead of 1937, she would have hobbled her way out of a dancing class while her teacher mopped his brow, shook his head and suggested she took lessons in working a computer. With no computers in 1940, she was fortunate enough to be able to use her own God-given talents.

Saying that, however, seems to suppose that it was all luck. It wasn't. Those talents were real. People bought copies of her record of 'Sentimental Journey' and young men in khaki, olive green or navy blue suits played them with tears in their eyes – tears were

Doris the young singer, in the late 1940s

in the eyes of their sweethearts, too – as they began journeys that were not in the least bit sentimental and from which they could never be sure they would ever return.

'Sentimental Journey' was Doris Day's first big hit. It was the first number she heard being played on nationally networked radio programmes. Wherever the band went on its one-night stands, Les Brown introduced his female vocalist and the kids out front demanded that she sang the song. When the band stopped at a diner for a snack on their way to a town none of them really wanted to be in, it was the tune everyone wanted to play on the jukebox. When she went back to her hotel at night, it was the song she heard on her own radio.

Of course, the record was Les Brown's. The 'vocal refrain', as they put it in those days, was by Doris Day. It was a name that got noticed. Nevertheless, devotees of Les Brown's band – the people who lined up for a dance or a show at which they performed simply because they were the ones who were performing – knew her name as well as they knew his. Certainly, they knew it as well as they knew the names of, say, Frances Langford and of Ray Eberlee when they sang with Glenn Miller, or Jo Stafford and a skinny youngster who sang with Tommy Dorsey, a kid called Frank Sinatra.

The Big Bands had never been bigger and it seemed as though, before long, there would be no name larger in the singing category than that of Doris Day.

Throughout the war years, Doris Day and Les Brown seemed to go together as easily as bacon and eggs or any of the other dishes they munched away at on the unsentimental journeys to and from the next gig. Bob Hope, who before long would have Les as his own resident band leader, liked 'Sentimental Journey' and other records of Doris's that he heard and considered taking her under his wing. It was Brown's idea. The bandleader knew that he was contemplating a replacement for Frances Langford who, after leaving Miller, went everywhere that Hope went, entertaining troops in the steaming jungles of the South Pacific or on the battlefronts of Italy or France. But he wanted a new face on the stage with him when he performed live – and a new voice for his radio shows.

The story has always been that they couldn't agree on money. There could be – and this is just speculation among people who knew the way that Hope operated – another explanation. A new girl working for America's most popular comedian was expected to perform other functions not initially specified in her contract. It is likely that Doris Day would not have wanted that.

Nevertheless, a year after their initial meeting, a deal was struck. Doris would sing with Bob – with no understanding of extra-curricular activities – and for ten times the sort of financial reward that had originally been talked about.

Looking back on that time years afterwards, she has said that she recognized just how bad a lot of those radio shows were, but Hope got the ratings and his staff told him how good he was. He seems to have thought she was pretty good, too. What he admired about her was her timing – the main requirement of a good comedian like Hope himself, but a characteristic not often related to singers. He said that she was a ballad singer above all, and ballad singers told stories.

Hope took to her like a comedian to a microphone. He called her 'JB', which stood for 'Jut Butt'. As he said: 'You could play bridge on her ass.' There's nothing on record to show that he actually did.

It was a good time for Doris to join Hope. They really did like each other.

'I think,' Melville Shavelson, Bob's chief writer, told me, 'he liked her unspoiled nature. She was very shy – and I think she still is. A lovely girl.'

In a snowstorm in Oklahoma City, she persuaded the highest-paid entertainer in America to go out on a sleigh ride with her – an adventure that only a girl from the likes of freezing Cincinnati could be expected to appreciate in its full glory. More important, he gave her some advice – she should be less reluctant to face live audiences. He himself always lived for an audience's response. But his advice was to have no effect. What Doris Day was able to achieve, she believed, was there for her to grab in front of a microphone or a camera.

Performers of an earlier generation would, until the end of their days, find that difficult to understand – particularly those who stood waiting for a piece of electronic equipment to get up and cheer, and never ceased to be depressed that it did not.

By then, Doris was big indeed. She made records of her own. She co-starred on other people's radio shows – which was the real sign that a performer had actually 'made it'. The guest star was always the big draw, not necessarily the one with his or her name above the billing. Jack Benny once told me how that worked: 'I'd give all the best lines to Bob Hope, Bing Crosby, Tony Martin, or whoever was my guest star and sometimes I didn't even get one good sentence to say. But the next day, people would say to each other at work, "Did you hear that joke or that song on the Jack Benny programme?" I couldn't ask for more.'

Doris appeared on the *Kraft Music Hall*, the show that Al Jolson hosted each week, and sang 'Put Your Arms Around Me, Honey' with him. His last line was 'Oh, Doris!' In the late 1940s, after the runaway success of, first, *The Jolson Story* and then, *Jolson Sings Again*, no performer could ask for more.

She could, however, have asked for much more in her private life – which, again, was not nearly as virginal as her later image and reputation would suggest. She began dating a tenor saxophone player and, years later, made no secret of the fact that they went to bed together and thoroughly enjoyed the experience.

His name was George Weidler and, she would say, they fell in love – without ever liking each other, or at least without her liking him. In fact, it appears she was happier with the situation than he was. They got married, decided that their home would be in Los Angeles – where he was working with CBS – even if it could only be in a trailer. But, eight months later, they were divorced.

They had tried to make it work. Both took up Christian Science and, for a time, that looked as though it might sort things out for them. But even when Doris thought that she would make a go of it, George had other ideas. It was he who phoned her with the news that it was all over.

But these were strange times. He allowed her to be the one to sue for divorce – on the grounds of his desertion.

As she would later tell a journalist: 'He was gentle and considerate and we had a strong physical attraction for each other, but I didn't realize that it takes much more than that to make a marriage work. We were apart for too long.'

Nevertheless, even after they had divorced, they still slept together. There would be bouts of passionate sex and that seemed enough to satisfy her.

Her ever-burgeoning career was pretty satisfying, too. She had a recording contract with Columbia – not one of those lush contracts that made young singers swoon, particularly when they were featured in a backstage film musical – but one that said if she ever made a record it had to be with them. It meant that she was in New York more often than she would have wanted to be. As Doris said, at heart she knew what the problem was: she was 'an old-fashioned girl' who just wanted to say yes when someone asked her to marry him.

But two broken marriages represented much more of a lost fantasy. 'My most persistent dream as a young girl was to get married and live happily ever after with a husband and children I could take care of and cook for. Even when I was young, I was not ambitious. I never had any drive in me.'

Both those statements need investigation. The first was the suggestion that she was not ambitious. Without ambition, she would never have left Cincinnati in the first place. No drive? Well, perhaps she didn't need it. She had a very nice voice that people liked to hear and when she was ready for them to hear it, there was frequently somebody around to help make it possible.

If only the life of Doris Day, young woman, would be half as successful, a fraction as rewarding, as that of Doris Day, performer. She missed the idea of a solid home life every bit as much as had her mother. But her strange and unnatural (for outsiders, that is) life didn't mean that she was separated from the people for whom she cared most. Whenever there was at least a week's stint in a city or town, Alma would bring Terry to come and stay with her. It wasn't a perfect way for a child to grow up, but at least he knew who his mother was. Al Jorden would have liked Terry to know who his father was, too. But Doris discouraged any meetings between her son and her ex-husband –

presumably because she didn't want the boy to find out *what* his father really was.

Who Terry's mother really was was going to be much less of a secret. She went to Hollywood.

She wasn't there to make films. Although her agent thought that was precisely what she should do, the men in the studios disagreed. The first producer who saw her didn't think the girl without make-up, the one in the unattractive sweater, was ready for the movies.

However, once in the film town, she was taken on as a restaurant singer – at a place called the Little Club. She sang 'Sentimental Journey', of course. She also sang whatever was top of the pops of the day like 'How About You?' and 'April Showers'. But she wasn't happy. She cried a lot.

And she decided to go back home to Cincinnati.

But before she was quite ready to go, she accepted the odd party invitation – like the one for the shindig at the home of the eminent songwriter, Jule Styne. There, she was persuaded to sing. And there, she was heard – by Styne and by his then partner Sammy Cahn. They were about to work on a new film. And they knew she was made to measure to star in it.

It's *Magic*

Sammy Cahn knew he had struck gold that night at Jule Styne's house. 'Struck gold,' he told me shortly before his death. 'I knew I had mined it and come up with the lode. Doris took some persuading to sing that night. She wasn't a very happy young lady. But I suggested that she tried "Embraceable You". Every girl singer did that, so if she couldn't manage a number like that, there wouldn't be much point in taking things any further. Well, she sang it. And she was just marvellous. I knew that she was the girl I wanted to sing my songs.'

There was one song in particular that he wanted Doris to perform, a number on which he thought she could work her own kind of magic. But he wasn't telling her about it. At that stage, the idea of giving away what was essentially a trade secret wouldn't have been at all clever. But what he did give away was the offer to introduce Ms Doris Day to the most prestigious director at Warner Bros.

This was Michael Curtiz, a man who shot to world fame years after his death – thanks to David Niven. Niven wrote two books of Hollywood memoirs and gave as the title of one, a phrase that Curtiz had used while shooting his film, *The Charge of the Light Brigade*. When it came to the time for a group of riderless chargers to be brought on, he shouted, 'Bring on the empty horses.'

As should now become clear, the Hungarian-born director mangled the English language with the same kind of dexterity that he used for making some of the most creative movies that the Warner studio had ever turned out. None was – or could be – greater than *Casablanca*. It was the high spot of an already very high career.

No one at Warner's pretended that *Romance on the High Seas* was going to be another *Casablanca* or even a notable film, but it was a 'stocking filler' for Curtiz, who was forming his own production company and needed products and stars to fill them. He had an arrangement with Warner Bros, for whom he had almost exclusively worked

With Jack Carson in *Romance on the High Seas*

in his distinguished career. If not a stocking filler, it would be a pot-boiler.

The very mention of the name of the male star, Jack Carson, instantly gave away the game. This was going to be a light, frothy comedy that also included a band singer in a sleazy night-club – for whom the idea of travel is a faraway dream. It is a dream that comes true when another woman suspects that her husband has a mistress and intends to spy on him. She suggests that a decoy is brought in – so that she can stay in New York and see whether her old man still has a mistress. Meanwhile, the husband has the same thoughts about his wife, employs a private eye on the ship – who, of course, gets the two women confused and 'discovers' the affair that she is having.

If that sounds complicated, one can only imagine the problems that Michael Curtiz had explaining it. Doris Day knocked on the door of the bungalow from which he operated on the Warner lot and he set about his explanations. And he explained something else, too: the part of the singer, the 'other woman', had originally been earmarked for Judy Garland. But Garland was in the midst of one of her perennial crises and couldn't make it. No Judy, so Betty Hutton was all but signed up. But Betty, a big star at the time, was pregnant and couldn't do it. So the part was up for grabs. Would Doris care to do a screen test?

There are now – and there certainly were then – girls who would give ten years of their lives for just such a question to be put to them, particularly if there was the likelihood of a positive outcome. Doris wasn't so sure. In fact, she later said that she cried throughout the interview. These were not tears of emotion at the notion of having achieved something so important, so early. She maintained it was simply because she was so unhappy in her personal life.

It was, she remembered, 'too much for me and the dam just sort of burst'.

As she also explained: 'Every time something like this happened, I always found myself in complete dejection. My husband and I had recently separated which did not help my mood.' She was also intimidated by Curtiz. 'Meeting big people like him scared me.'

She knew she had behaved 'like a frightened schoolgirl', but it was all in character. As she would say, she always cried at all the big things that had happened in her life. And then, it wasn't so very terrible. The astonished Curtiz was fatherly, she always recalled, and perhaps that was what she had always needed most of all – Les Brown knew that.

She did manage to sing 'Embraceable You' to the great director. As a result, he was more sure than ever that he wanted to see her in a test with Jack Carson. 'I want for you to make screen tests for me. Don't cry. That is no way for an actress to behave. I like you. I like your voice. Everthink vill be hokay.'

Just how 'hokay', it didn't take long to find out.

She made the test and Carson himself telephoned her to say that she had been not just 'hokay' but sensational. Yes, it was true that about a hundred other young women had tested – yes, a hundred – but he was sure that Doris was the one who would make it. He was right. Curtiz liked her as much as Carson had and offered her the part.

That phone call changed the life of Doris Day – and there are numerous fans out there who would still say that it changed theirs, too.

From that moment on, the nice homespun girl who, sad though it was, had had little chance to be anything of the kind, was no longer a band singer. For the first time in her life – at least since she had wet her pants in that kindergarten show – she was acting. And from then on, most of the singing that she did was going to be in front of a camera. It took a little time for her to realize that it was going to be a medium that was made for her. She said she couldn't understand why Curtiz and Warner's were so happy to see her. She didn't look like a film star. Which was precisely true.

It would be nice to think that she was the trouper everyone knew that, at heart, she was. Unfortunately, the most famous crying scene in Hollywood – at least since Louis B. Mayer's frequent habit of sacking his stars while dabbing his eyes with a handkerchief – continued on the set.

Doris was known as 'Miss Lachrymose'. Not even the wit of the third co-star Oscar Levant could bring her out of depressions that didn't exactly halt production, but threatened to do so. He was the one who would say he remembered her well – from the time before she became a virgin. That was not a statement she enjoyed hearing. 'It was such a load of junk,' she later said. 'After all, I was married with a child at the time.'

But the public didn't know that. And her films didn't give the impression of a woman who knew – to quote Sammy Cahn again – what went where. Nobody, however, really thought that Levant's quip was anything but a good joke about a pretty good singer.

In *Romance on the High Seas*, she got to sing the Sammy Cahn–Jule Styne song for which she would weave her special kind of Doris Day spell, to coin a phrase. 'It's Magic' was to be the hit of the film, as well as one of the great standards of the age.

'You always hope that a song is going to be successful, but, of course, you can never be sure that it will be,' Cahn told me. 'You always hope that one song at least in a picture will grab people's attention, but you never know which one – if you are that lucky – it will be. When Doris sang "It's Magic", I took a bet with Jule that that would be the one. This freckle-faced kid who had never been in a movie before did everything right.'

From her point of view, it was lucky too. The film will never be one of those that she would look back upon as her greatest ever performance, the one in which the dialogue shone from every page of the script. The critics weren't universally approving. One wrote: 'Miss Day looks as if she has been hit in the face with paint from a spray gun.' Ironical, that, since she had indeed been sprayed. It was an attempt to remove her freckles – although it sometimes looked as if it had merely painted them on.

There were no such inhibitions about 'It's Magic'. And, it has to be said, few about Doris Day herself. *Picturegoer*'s Mabel Stonier commented in July 1949: 'She's the Day after tomorrow – the latest and most promising recruit to the not so thick ranks of feminine songsters possessing a face, figure, voice and personality tailored to fit the catchy crochets of those musicals that Hollywood does so well.'

That said a great deal about the big newcomer to the cinema in general – and about the movie musical in particular, a genre that at the time seemed as if it was going to be around for ever.

Nobody then knew that it wouldn't be there for ever – or that within the first five years of the new decade this particular songster would achieve so much without singing a note.

What was obvious – and Mabel Stonier caught it perfectly – was the breadth of what Doris Day achieved. 'She can put over a slow, lush torch song with a depth of feeling that would wring the withers of the sourest anti-swing fan, then switch to a hot-rhythm number with the ease and finesse of a Crosby.'

That in itself said a lot – although the comparison didn't seem right. Crosby was the nice-'n'-easy crooner of the age. He had long left hot rhythm behind. What was true about the comment was that whatever was current and 'hot' in 1949, Doris Day was there in the forefront.

Another critic described her as 'a combination of Judy Garland, Betty Hutton and Dolores Gray'. That wasn't good enough. When Doris Day sang 'It's Magic', she was exhibiting a talent that was all her own.

This was the girl who sang 'My Dream Is Yours' and made it sound like a lullaby. Then she belted out 'Canadian Capers' and you realized what style really was.

But it was 'It's Magic' that set the Atlantic on fire. It became such a big chart-topper – or, to use the more elegant phraseology of the time, spent so long at the top of the hit parade – that when the movie opened in Britain, it had a new title, *It's Magic*. Sammy Cahn was pleased. It was, after all, 'his' title. That was real success. Doris Day didn't do badly out of it, either.

Suddenly, instead of going back to Cincinnati, she had a movie contract and a record that was top of the hit parade. The executives at Warner Bros chatted over the best steaks in California in Jack L. Warner's private dining-room and agreed that Doris Day ought to go into a new movie just as quickly as a sound stage could be dusted off and the lens of a camera given an extra touch of polish.

She was an unlikely star. But that was what she was. A star. And the studio publicists played on the point. Doris Day spent her money on clothes and perfume, they reported. Only a star rated such rubbish, but there were hundreds of thousands of young girl fans who flooded the chain stores looking for clothes of the kind she wore – and wrote asking for details of her favourite scent. If the perfume could drive the men wild at Warner Bros, what could it do for their own love lives?

Tea for Two

The fan magazines were grabbing at all the news they could get of this bright new personality on the screen – aided by a great deal of nonsensical publicity that the Warner outfit were convinced sold their movies.

One thing was true about the image they thought they had to promote, if not create. She was the kind of girl high school teachers used to like to encourage their students to emulate. The Catholic League of Decency was only too delighted to give *Romance on the High Seas* and anything else with the Doris Day name on it, their coveted seal of approval. Yet this, of course, could be a disadvantage, too. So, the more sophisticated journals and the kind of radio programmes that went out in what Sinatra liked to call the wee, small hours of the morning, were given a slightly different spin on the girl from Ohio: she not only sang nice, sweet songs like 'It's Magic' and 'Sentimental Journey', but get her on a good evening, with a nice accompaniment and she was the best torch singer in the business.

It would be a few years before *Love Me or Leave Me*, but she wasn't beyond encouraging the thought, either. Yet Jack Warner didn't like it. And why should he? His studio had spent a fortune on fabricating a certain kind of star for the end of the 1940s and he was not about to lose that investment by making audiences wonder what sort of actress they were about to see.

It was publicity, publicity, publicity, all the way. One thing was clear, Barney Rapp's choice of name for Ms Kappelhoff had been inspired – if for no other reason than the gift it gave to the headline writers. All over America, and then in Britain, articles were headed 'Dawn of a Bright Day' or 'It's a Bright Day' or perhaps 'Day Break'. It didn't matter if it meant very much or not. You had a word like 'Day' to play with and you took advantage of the fact.

Whatever the publicity people wanted, she gave. 'Make a few jokes,' said one PR

Co-starring with Ronald Reagan in *The Winning Team*

man – and then primed reporters that this apparently virginal creature had a wicked sense of humour. 'Are you afraid of the dark?' asked one reporter. 'It depends who's in it,' she replied, and every press man in the room had to hold his sides. They were simple days. So simple that reporters supposedly really wanted to know that she played gin rummy as well as hockey and hated talking on the phone (a mistake saying that because it played havoc with any idea that this was the girl next door who liked doing what girls who lived next door liked to do).

Not surprisingly, the cats (and worse animal impersonators) and dogs began to fight over her. Louella Parsons and Hedda Hopper, the two prize bitches of the Hollywood gossip columns, went on the attack. Hollywood moguls loved and hated the columnists in equal measure. They loved them when they said nice things about their stars (usually inspired by tiny inconsequential gifts like a new Cadillac or a mink coat) and they feared them when they knew that something might have offended the dear ladies.

What it was that worried Ms Parsons in particular has never been certain. It might just have been jealousy, a feeling that the young woman was just too lucky and had hit the big time much too soon. Whatever it was, this powerhouse of a journalist went on to the attack – principally to say that the girl wasn't all peaches and cream and shouldn't be treated as though she were.

'Dodo,' she told her readers, mockingly, was a money grabber (she was making $750 a week – not bad money for a twenty-three-year-old in 1947, but not exactly in the money-grabbing star class). Not just that, she was always late on the set. To a professional actress, that was verging on the insulting. Being late for work conjured up impressions of Doris Day being another temperamental Judy Garland – and no studio wanted that. It was also untrue and potentially libellous, but you didn't sue Louella Parsons and live to talk about it.

The stories of her falling in love with a certain other Warner star, Ronald Reagan (and just imagine what a difference that combination might have made to the Doris Day of the 1980s), were also false. It was true that she did go on dates with the future President – at a time when his only ambitions seem to have been directed towards getting a decent part. But that's all they were, dates. Years later, when a paper reported an affair between the two of them, she sued.

It was a time when Reagan's political gaze went no further than heading the Screen Actors' Guild (which he did twice), but most of the stories were again engineered by the Warner Bros publicity men, people who always saw the potential of getting two of their stars to date each other. (In a 1983 interview, Doris said: 'If we had married, just think, we could have used the poster from our last movie for the campaign.') But they would do more serious work together – at least, they would some time in the future.

She also went out with Jack Carson, for much the same reason as she dated Reagan – at least in that case they were plugging the same film.

In 1949, that film was *My Dream Is Yours*, which also did good service to the title song. It was another fairly inconsequential movie, but Doris did well in it as a young radio singer who had a small son to support. The notion of single mothers wasn't the most popular one among the fan and women's magazines, but starring in a film that almost told her own story was a nice way of preparing a growing number of fans for the fact that not everything was entirely wonderful at home for Doris – and yet, look how marvellous she is.

Hollywood always liked to say that whatever else it did, it mirrored life – even when it didn't – and they weren't going to allow an opportunity like this to get away. Of course, they stressed – over and over again – that Ms Day's predicament was none of her own doing and, through it all, she had coped superbly. Just wait for her next film – and you wouldn't know that anything could possibly be wrong.

There was a fair amount of crying in her next movie, too. *Young Man with a Horn*, however, was a very different sort of film. The picture – called *Young Man of Music* in Britain – featured the young Kirk Douglas, given every opportunity now, straight from his brilliant performance as a boxer in *Champion*, to show not just how beefy, but also how sensitive and tormented he could be. Doris, for her part, was given her first chance to show just how good an actress she was.

She and Douglas didn't get on terribly well, but it didn't show in the movie.

It was 1950 and the emotional story of a disturbed trumpeter still able to produce the sweetest sounds this side of heaven was a gritty mix of reality, steamy romance and the sort of music that made the average movie-goer want to go straight home and wind up the handle on his gramophone.

Doris made an album of songs from the picture, one of the first LPs to cash in on the previously unexplored goldmine that the new medium offered, and it sold like hot gramophone records.

The picture did have one effect that a psychiatrist might just have predicted. Doris being portrayed as falling in love with a musician brought back all those painful memories of her life with Al Jorden. Nevertheless, she seems to have had the strength to deal with it – although it would be a long time before she recognized the fact. Actually, she would say that it was the presence of one the greats of popular music, Hoagy Carmichael, appearing in character as the slightly cynical pianist, that helped her get over the obvious associations with Jorden.

Before long, she knew she was on to a winner. Indeed, if all the Doris Day films that followed had been anything like as drama ridden (even if, like this one, a certain degree of the feminine sex appeal had had to be shared with Lauren Bacall, playing what was billed at the time as the 'society temptress') this mixture of drama and music might have been a highly acceptable formula for a young actress/singer embarking on the perfect career. But both Michael Curtiz and Warner Bros had other ideas.

This story, loosely based on the tortured career of Bix Beiderbecke, did not represent the sort of future they had in mind for Doris. Had she made more pictures like this both she and her future in show business would have looked very different. As it was, the young men of America went for her in a big way. Troops sweating in the summer and freezing in the winter of the war in Korea all but adopted her. She was, they decided, the girl 'we would most like to take a slow boat to the States with'.

They did it three other times in that mid-century year. *It's a Great Feeling* was not one of the movies that gave rise to such emotions. Melville Shavelson, who with his partner Jack Rose wrote what could loosely be described as the script of this picture, does not exactly put it down as one of the high spots of his own career, either. 'It was a picture made by Warner Bros on the cheap. It used every contract artist around at the time on the Warner lot, without having to make a single stick of new scenery.'

Shavelson and Rose made Doris a girl from Hicksville who comes to Hollywood, lands a job as a waitress in the studio commissary and who, of course, is discovered and becomes a star.

When Errol Flynn appeared as her bridegroom – whose identity is only revealed as he lifts her veil to kiss her – that was all audiences wanted to know. They did know it was a terrible film, but they enjoyed it just the same. Warner's had to turn out – quite literally – a new film every week, but they were guaranteed showings at their own theatres, so that was hardly a problem. Before long, Hollywood would change and Doris Day would be there to reap the benefit, although she wasn't yet thinking about that.

In this, as in *My Dream Is Yours* and, of course, *Romance on the High Seas*, she was paired with Jack Carson – a partnership which, looking back on it now, seems unlikely. She was the small-town girl who wanted to believe only the good in people, he specialized in playing sophisticated dolts who wouldn't have stopped if they ran over their own mothers. Yet they hit it off beautifully – and she would always say how

With Kirk Douglas in *Young Man with a Horn*

grateful she was for the tips that he gave her. In fact, she said she always thought Carson had been a huge influence on her – which is nice to hear in a business that specializes in revealing all, years later, undoing all the publicity that accompanied them in their early success. Carson was the one who taught her how to win the battle of the camera – where to move, how to ensure the best shots. If he did that – allowed her to

Hitting the high notes in *It's a Great Feeling*

get the best shots, sometimes to his cost – he was a much nicer guy than his screen image seemed to suggest.

And he was doing it at the expense of his own career. The better known and more admired she became, the less enthusiasm there was likely to be for anyone else. He didn't seem to mind.

But Doris Day was the big new star at Warner's at what was to be close to the end of the studio contract system, and *It's a Great Feeling* was seen as a perfect vehicle for her to sing a couple of songs. Her main contribution was 'Blame My Absent-Minded Heart'. Not the most inspired Doris Day number ever, and certainly not a notable addition to the Sammy Cahn–Jule Styne songbook, but it went off well enough with that growing coterie now known as Doris Day fans.

Besides which, people enjoyed the chance to spot their favourite stars in cameo roles. This time, they had the opportunity to fix their eyes on a variety of contributors to *Who's Who* in Hollywood, ranging from Danny Kaye to Joan Crawford with names like Gary Cooper, Ronald Reagan and Sidney Greenstreet, the fat man of *The Maltese Falcon* and *Casablanca*, thrown in.

The second movie that got the Korea boys salivating turned out to be the start of a new genre, and it worked as beautifully as anything that Doris ever did. *Tea for Two* was made in what the trailers would have described as 'the glory of Technicolor', used the latest sound techniques and was up to date enough in its costumes and settings to excite couples in the back rows of cinemas all over the world whenever they chose to look up at the screen from the really exciting business at hand.

Even so, the picture represented unbridled nostalgia from the moment the opening titles faded. It was an update of the 1920s stage musical, *No No Nanette*, complete with most of the numbers from the Vincent Youmans–Irving Caesar score, not least of all the title number. That was the one that Caesar wrote as a 'cod lyric' in the space of minutes and then found that he couldn't improve upon. It would have been difficult to have improved on the formula either – plainly planned by Warner's to cash in on the desire of Korean War-weary audiences for the good things of life they still remembered from just a quarter of a century earlier. There have been many criticisms of that sort of musical over the years, but few could say that this story of an heiress who invests in a show and then becomes a big Broadway star herself didn't turn out to be their cup of tea (for two, of course). It marked Doris's first teaming with Gordon MacRae, and they looked good together on the big screen.

The time had come to establish what this star was going to be most famous for. It was Marty Melcher, her agent, who was responsible for making sure that the Doris Day image was given a supercharge. And, before long, Melcher would be much more of an influence in her life.

Melcher had a reputation as a man not to be trusted with other people's money. There were Melcher clients, like the Andrews Sisters, who worried about the stake that he took in their careers. Doris, however, didn't worry too much about him. It would prove to be yet another of those mistakes that she would be as good at making as the films in which she starred.

Melcher had taken over from his partner Al Levy as her agent – a nice twist, that. When Levy had that job, Melcher said he failed to see any great potential in the young blonde with the white teeth. In fact, he put it rather more strongly than that. 'Get rid of that dame,' he said. 'She's not worth bothering with.'

However it didn't take long for him to change his view. He saw Doris in the office and admired her trim figure. He saw *Tea for Two* and realized she had more than a little talent to offer. And there was something else. Whatever Al Levy had, Melcher wanted, too.

He especially wanted the object of Levy's latest enthusiasm – Doris. Levy would

Doris Day

In *Tea for Two*, Doris's first partnership with Gordon MacRae

have done anything to get her into bed, if not into a register office. He may not have known that Marty had similar ideas – and ones that Doris was more likely to accept. He and Ms Day were soon, as they later said in Hollywood, an 'item'. But his ideas were also affected by what he believed was his business acumen. He took on the task of co-producer of her films to prove the point (a double job that would later be ruled illegal). At the same time, he fired Levy from the firm they ran together – and changed the locks on his office door to emphasize the fact.

He took Doris under his professional wing and then allowed nature to take its course. She married Marty on her twenty-seventh birthday in April 1951. Again, it was a civil ceremony (Melcher had been born Jewish, news that wouldn't have pleased Mr Kappelhoff), not the romantic white wedding she might have dreamed of as a little girl.

'City Hall, New York City. City Hall, New Jersey. City Hall, Los Angeles. I have impeccable taste in weddings,' she commented.

He had popped the question, she later revealed, by standing with her in front of a furniture store window and telling her where he would place a chair they saw. 'That would look good in our living-room,' he said. 'No,' she replied, 'the dining-room.'

That was the proposal and she accepted.

They hadn't planned a honeymoon, but when reporters mobbed them, they fled to the mountains behind Los Angeles to escape for a few days.

It was the start of what seemed to be a wonderfully happy relationship. He taught her how to relax, she would say. He ended her chain-smoking when things were getting her down. He told her to start trusting people – which was an amazing statement, considering the fact that he himself trusted no one and practically no one trusted him.

But he looked after her interests like a mother hen watching over her chickens. He adopted Terry, the son Doris had had with Al Jorden. Before long, Terry would take his name. When he and Doris were seen together, it was as a happily married couple – which for Doris Day had not been a usual circumstance at all.

Melcher wasn't like the men she appeared with on screen. He just wasn't as good looking as any of them (except possibly Jack Carson). Doris knew that, but comforted herself by saying: 'Plain men are the best providers. They give a woman more material comforts and loyalty, develop their personalities, give more thought to their jobs than to impressing others. Handsome men are often selfish and inconsiderate – or are in love with themselves.'

Marty tried to show he was more in love with Doris, but it became obvious fairly early on that he realized she was going to be a very good meal ticket.

That being the case, he wanted to be sure that going to see a Doris Day picture ensured you knew the kind of movie you were about to view. He made it his ambition to see that a trademark was stamped on all Doris Day products. The clever thing would have been to do so without making her totally typecast, although that would be an ambition more difficult to achieve. There were going to be times when her perpetual virginity could be a handicap, so there would be a narrow tightrope for her to walk – between being so sugary her work would be banned to diabetics and giving the sort of wholesome performances for which she was already famous.

That being so, he was guiding her career to make sure she didn't slip off the rope. Sometimes she would still slip, but less frequently now.

On *Moonlight Bay*

Things were beginning to look good. But it took time for her to get into her stride. It took time, too, for Warners to totally agree with that trademark idea. Until studio executives – and Jack Warner himself in particular – could analyse whether *Tea for Two* had been truly an order they wanted to take up, they were still experimenting.

That could be the only reason for *West Point Story*, which co-starred James Cagney. If Doris Day and Cagney seemed an improbable teaming at the time, the excuse was that the improbable was Hollywood's stock-in-trade. A few years along the way, they would prove to be a very successful pair indeed, but at the outset, *West Point Story* didn't have much promise at all. It certainly didn't for the other woman in the movie, Virginia Mayo. As she told me: 'Doris Day wanted her husband to get me out and her in. She wanted to be the only female and to get me out of the picture and combine our roles. She wanted to be alone in all her pictures, but in this case didn't get her way. Jimmy wanted me in it.'

It was the tale of the staging of a musical at the military academy. Doris sang and Cagney snarled and audiences hoped she would return to something not too different from *Tea for Two*. But not just yet.

With her third 1951 movie, *Storm Warning*, she didn't sing at all. Warner's took the risk of not only letting her have a dramatic role, but gave her one with a story line as contentious as anything that Hollywood was turning out at the time.

America was still heavily divided on the race issue, but *Storm Warning* dealt openly – and bravely – with the Ku Klux Klan and all that the hooded cross-burning bigots represented. There was murder and every other kind of violence imaginable – all of it put under the magnifying lenses of the camera in a film in which Doris played the younger sister of Ginger Rogers. As for Ginger, she looked as though she had never

**With Gene Nelson, James Cagney, Virginia Mayo
and Gordon MacRae in *West Point Story***

danced a step in her life – and was just as effective. Doris herself might have felt happy to stretch her dramatic wings, and the studio system had proved it could be flexible, but stories about the Klan were not the reason paying customers went to see Doris Day movies and Marty was the first to realize the fact.

They still cried out for a new *Tea for Two*. Before long, their wishes were granted. The new stories were slight, but they showed the young Doris Day at her very best. What was more, they appealed to more of a cross-section of the population than possibly could have been imagined when the ideas for movies called *Lullaby of*

**A non-singing Doris and a non-dancing Ginger Rogers
with Steve Cochran in *Storm Warning***

Broadway, On Moonlight Bay and, a couple of years later, *By the Light of the Silvery Moon* first came up for 'pitching' sessions.

It was, of course, before the rock era, a time when the notion of a hip-swivelling Elvis Presley was nobody's idea of entertainment, but the post-war generation of teenagers was already the mainstay of the cinema industry. That being so, how anyone thought of using the titles of ancient songs for modern sophisticated films was one of the Hollywood mysteries of the early 1950s. But it was going to be a trend (and the reason soon became apparent) and a by-product of that trend would be establishing the very Doris Day trademark that her husband craved.

It took some time for people to understand why it was happening. Television was just dawning as an important entertainment medium, yet here was a studio with a big new star taking what was seemingly a retrogressive step.

On the other hand, this was a step in colour in an otherwise black and white age. And the films were good. They were also enjoyable to a degree that only the box-office could properly demonstrate.

It had been a long time since the Harry Warren–Al Dubin number 'Lullaby of Broadway' had been a hit. Yet when Doris sang it in the film of that name, it seemed amazingly up to date – particularly when it was featured in one of those roller-coaster close-ups that Hollywood liked so much at the time. Harry Warren once told me: 'Every writer wants to see his songs take on new life, but it doesn't just happen. You need the right setting and the right performer. The film and Doris Day were that.'

She and the audiences had reason to be grateful for David Butler's direction of yet another seemingly tired old story about putting on a Broadway show – although Doris would say that the amount of work going into the dance numbers was exhausting. Especially so for a girl who not all those many years before had spent so long in plaster and who had believed she would never dance again.

But it all worked out. The title number wasn't the only old song given new life in the film. There was also 'Just One of Those Things', which became an upbeat Day classic, and 'Zing Went the Strings of my Heart'.

On Moonlight Bay was out of the same mould. It brought Doris and Gordon MacRae together again in another story written by Melville Shavelson and Jack Rose.

Talking to Shavelson, the reason for using a song title long past its sell-by date became apparent. As he told me: 'Warner's had a whole lot of songs in their publishing department that weren't selling any more. It was Jack [Warner's] idea that it would give new life to them if they became film titles. The story is that he would go to the music catalogue with a tooth pick, close his eyes and point it at a title.

'This time, he picked "On Moonlight Bay" and told us to write a film with that name.'

Nobody suggested that it would have to have anything whatever to do with the story-line. That was going to be Messrs Shavelson and Rose's department.

'I had always loved the Penrod and Sam stories as a kid – the ones about two boys, their dog and their sister. Since I knew this was going to be a film for Doris Day, I suggested making the sister the biggest part.' Jack Warner took some convincing,

In full song again in *Lullaby of Broadway*

though. The studio owned the original Penrod and Sam copyrights and years before had made a film about the characters. 'It was so bad,' he told his writers, 'they still haven't got the stink out of the theatres.'

But the mogul finally agreed – and then had a violent row with Shavelson, who had allowed his sense of humour to get the better of him. 'I said that the brothers and their dog should be called Harry, Jack and Albert' – the names of the Warner brothers themselves. After almost physically throwing the pair out of his office, Warner eventually accepted the idea – but not the names of the brothers and their dog.

With Gordon MacRae for the classic duet in *On Moonlight Bay*

Doris sang 'On Moonlight Bay', which conveniently became the name of the local amusement park. It also became a turn-of-the-century love story that formed part of another Hollywood tradition – the girl next door with the pony tail who blossoms to be the love of the boy next door, the one who inevitably wore the striped blazer and straw hat.

This was pure nostalgia. It confirmed that Warner Bros knew what they were doing – in virtually inventing a kind of picture with which they then became reasonably sure that the public would run. For a time it seemed that this was going to be the way Doris

Singing better than ever, with Danny Thomas (at right) in *I'll See You in My Dreams*

Day's career was going to go. Inevitably, she didn't like the notion of typecasting – for whichever kindly spin was put on it, this was precisely what it was – but it was a hell of a successful type in which to be cast.

It was said often enough that *On Moonlight Bay* was *Meet Me in St Louis* revisited, but Doris Day wasn't in that earlier Judy Garland picture, so it was different enough. She was now twenty-seven, perhaps a little too old to be featured as a tomboy baseball player, but once she agreed to get into a dress, she looked pretty and sounded as good in this as in anything she had done. Gordon MacRae's duet with Doris of the title song became another one of those – well, let's say it – classics.

The trouble with typecasting is that stars think they are never going to get out of it.

Doris was luckier than most. *I'll See You in My Dreams* was, like *Storm Warning*, in black and white, but it was back to the old formula – if, for once, she was in what was supposedly a true story. The movie was based on the life of the songwriter Gus Kahn and, of course, featured some of his big hits, ranging from the title song to 'It Had to Be You' and 'Toot Toot Tootsie'. It followed all the old biopic formulae. And it made her one of the two top money-makers in American cinema.

In this, she was the girl from the good family who didn't want her to marry a songwriter. She did all the rather exasperating things young ladies were supposed to do to discourage an unsuitable suitor – until, inevitably, she marries him, loves him to distraction, and shares all the tough as well as the great things in his life. Of course, she sings his songs – frequently on first sight of the sheet music. That was what people expected and that was what they got. Danny Thomas was superb as Gus Kahn and Doris had rarely been better – singing better than ever, playing a dramatic role without the music spoiling her now obvious acting talents.

She was now established as a Warner's star. It was also a good time for Doris's international career. She was singing songs that became top-sellers even when she hadn't featured them in her movies. In 1952, she had her first British triumph in what was the first-ever British hit parade with her song, 'Sugarbush', a South African folk song brought to Britain by Eve Boswell. In the second hit parade, her version of 'My Love and Devotion' entered at number ten. Another huge hit that year was 'When I Fall in Love'.

It was also the year when it became obvious that other entertainers were clamouring to appear with her – a mark of arrival, if ever there were one. The top male singing star was then the ever-weeping Johnnie Ray, so it made sense for both of them to combine their talents in numbers like 'Let's Walk Thataway', which can be fairly assumed to have done very little for her career or her talents.

The film *Starlift* (or *Starlift Bay*, an alternative title) wasn't as exciting as that record. Or, to rephrase that, it was a total, unmitigated disaster. The consolation, as far as Day fans were concerned, was that she only had a cameo role in this movie about stars entertaining at an Air Force base where the troops were all the time on the move to Korea. It was another one of those portmanteau films that Warner Bros liked so much. Of course they liked them; they gave them a wonderful chance to use all their contract artists and all their sets in one movie. Among those she joined in this can't-forget-quickly-enough epic were Gordon MacRae, Virginia Mayo, Gene Nelson, James Cagney, Gary Cooper, Phil Harris and Jane Wyman – in other words, virtually everyone who was around at the time. Even Louella Parsons made an appearance.

Why did Doris ever agree to make some of the films she was being told to show up for? The answer she gave was pretty basic. 'Everybody was saying to me, "What do you know about it? A deal's a deal." '

The truth was, they were deals she didn't want.

After *Starlift*, *The Winning Team* had to be better, although making that judgement was stretching the imagination somewhat. With the benefit of 20-20 hindsight, it is a museum piece – Doris Day teamed with a future President of the United States. Doris liked Ronald Reagan – if only because he loved taking her dancing. Her views on his acting abilities have been less publicly expressed. Playing the woman in the life of a telephone linesman who became a baseball star wasn't calculated to bring Doris Day fans demanding seats at the box-office. They thought that the experimenting was over. They knew what they wanted – a chance to hear Doris sing and look pretty as she flashed both those teeth and the smile around them.

Their prayers were about to be answered. There would be more musicals that showed the former Ms Kappelhoff doing what she did best.

Melcher knew that *Tea for Two*, *Lullaby of Broadway* and *On Moonlight Bay* were the sort of pictures people liked most. But, if it weren't for a regular supply of Doris Day records, they might have started asking if she knew any new songs.

April in Paris reinforced the thought – it also gave her a co-star of an earlier generation, the straw man from *The Wizard of Oz*, Ray Bolger. But Bolger was left in no doubt that the star was Doris Day and she was very definitely on the way up. Nevertheless, Bolger's dance routines helped make up for a fairly poor product.

That they did is one of the miracles of the film business. Doris said in her autobiography that she didn't enjoy making the film – largely because the director David Butler accused Bolger of trying to upstage her throughout the production.

In this film, about a chorus girl mistakenly invited to an American arts festival in the French capital (that shows how desperate Warner's were for a good plot line), she was meant to be the victim of all the male wiles that young girls were supposed to be warned about by their mothers. But she won out in the story just as she did in the public's reaction. True Doris Day fans were not at all surprised.

If the public had any doubts about *April in Paris* – and it could have done better at the box-office – *By the Light of the Silvery Moon* was the sort of Doris Day picture they had been wanting since *On Moonlight Bay*. Gordon MacRae was there again and the formula was just the same – another early twentieth-century story, with colour, long skirts, straw hats and great music.

Actually, it was an acknowledged sequel to *On Moonlight Bay*. Doris and Gordon played the same characters, except that this time she didn't play baseball and he exchanged his blazer for a World War One Army uniform.

Looking back now, it is clear that this was a completely new development in the

April in Paris, with co-star Ray Bolger (at left)

Hollywood story – and the name Doris Day was firmly stamped all over it. It had never happened before, not even in the other periods of nostalgia that frequently invaded the film community like a reappearing virus.

Here was a young, vivacious singer-actress who was as essential a part of the 1950s as Eisenhower in the White House, the Ford Edsel (only with much more success) and the hula-hoop. In fact, she was earning her money in a time warp. Everything she did on film seemed to be parked in an age she barely knew.

On the set of *By the Light of the Silvery Moon*, with
Marty Melcher and one of her best friends

The truth was that she made the 1920s and 1930s a lot more romantic and palatable than they ever were in reality. When she sang 'Lullaby of Broadway' in the film of that name, it was no paean to the by now seedy thoroughfare that the theatre street had become. For her audience, the lights of the street gleamed and so did the magic that the film made it out to be.

Broadway in the hands – and voice – of Doris Day was as clean and as romantic as the dresses she wore. The voice, aided by the latest orchestrations and the finest state-of-art sound systems, made her audiences yearn for an age that history dictated should have been remembered for the Depression, dust storms and the onset of war.

They were charming, unusual vehicles for an equally charming, unusual talent. It took some time for the penny to drop that this was, indeed, a series of movies they were being invited to watch. The biggest demonstration of its success was that when this collection of nostalgic offerings became, like the period they covered, a thing of the past, people wanted more of the same. But how long could it really last? The studio, and Doris herself, thought that the time had come to move on.

There was another visit to the past on the horizon, but this was going to be different – and more successful than she could possibly have imagined.

It was going to be another milestone.

Calamity Jane

Calamity Jane was indeed another one of those milestones. It was one of three films Doris made when she was thirty, but more important than any of them – in fact, more important than anything she had done to date.

Ask the average moviegoer to name a Doris Day film and chances are this movie about the nineteenth-century Wild West will be at the top of the list. And for all sorts of marvellously acceptable reasons.

Again, it was a demonstration of the tightrope walk turning into marathon success. Once more, it was the tomboy Doris who eventually blossoms into the beautiful lady that her fans liked to think she always was. Some of the more arty critics have drawn similarities between *Calamity Jane* and *The Taming of the Shrew*. The comparison couldn't be less appropriate. The Jane in the title was never a horrific character. Kate in Shakespeare's play was always resolutely feminine (even when in *Kiss Me Kate*, the musical based on the play, she sings 'I Hate Men'), always appears in attractive dresses. On the other hand, you never wanted to take Jane on your knee and slap her behind for being so uncompromising and domineering. This was a girl who enjoyed wearing masculine clothes in the middle of a mining town, who loved playing boys' games, but who, when she meets the love of her life, simply melts. And Doris Day always melted better than most other actresses of her generation (a generation when a female player would never have wanted to be called an 'actor').

Plainly, the picture was cashing in on her fame. It also did a pretty good job of following on the success of *Annie Get Your Gun* and allowing Doris to beat Betty Hutton at her own game – the one of proving that, yes, a girl could get a man with a gun. The man was the same in both movies – Howard Keel. The Frank Butler of *Annie* was virtually interchangeable with the Wild Bill Hickok of *Calamity*.

And, strangely enough, so was the music. Which was one hell of a compliment to

In the ground-breaking and memorable *Calamity Jane*

With Howard Keel in *Calamity Jane*

the writers Sammy Fain and Paul Webster. Irving Berlin had never done better than he had with his score for *Annie Get Your Gun* – virtually every song became a hit. By then, of course, the man who had written 3,000 songs (many of which are among the world's greatest standards) was merely doing what comes naturally – to coin a phrase, or at least an *Annie* song title. Now, Fain and Webster's tunes for *Calamity Jane* experienced the same fate, which is not an achievement to be sniffed at. But it was Doris's interpretation of them that made the songs the triumphs they were.

'Secret Love' won an Oscar for best song of 1953 (and stayed in the charts for twenty-two weeks, after heading them for three). 'The Black Hills of Dakota' was top of the pops for just as long as it took practically every record pressed to sell out.

And that was the real secret of the Doris Day success – making the films in which she starred big simply because she was starring in them and then exploiting them to increase her already exalted status as a record maker.

The soldier's cap she wore in the film was of the US Cavalry, and the scenes in which she wore it were among the few times in *Calamity Jane* in which she had a clean face. Yet she had all the chances in the world to demonstrate what was undoubtedly a Doris Day knack – of being able to play a tough cookie no man would want to look at twice and yet in the flash of a projector's beam overwhelm them with her latent femininity.

It worked wondrously. Marty Melcher couldn't have been happier. That movie safely in the can, when nothing seemingly could have gone wrong, Marty directed her towards another one of those occasional switches of subject which should never have materialized. Everyone makes mistakes, but *Lucky Me* was not just inappropriately titled – she would have been far luckier to have turned it down flat, even risking suspension from Warner Bros – it could have been a disaster. As she herself said, she was amazed at how bad it was. But in the days of the studio system, you were tied by a contract and you did as you were told – unless you wanted a confrontation with the boss, which in her case was always a fruitless operation.

In her autobiography, she said that she never considered herself a star – which was why she always hid in a corner at parties. It was also, she said, why she had had the temerity to argue with Jack Warner himself when the Warner Bros boss tried to get her to make a film she didn't want to do. He said that was what stars always tried to do – mind his business; she replied that she didn't consider herself a star, just an actress who wanted to do her job properly.

And that she always was. Even when the films weren't that marvellous, even when they were downright terrible (and some were just that) she could be depended on to work as hard as the professional that she always was.

Even in *Lucky Me*. There was one good song in the picture; 'I Speak to the Stars' – something she did a lot of in the movie itself, to stars like Robert Cummings and Phil Silvers (taking a break from *Bilko*). The story of a group of entertainers stranded in Florida – others included Eddie Foy Jr and Nancy Walker – turned out to be merely forgettable. What was lucky about it was that Doris didn't suffer. There are just a few stars who can afford to make lousy pictures – like the late Laurence Olivier, Sean Connery and Michael Caine – without it affecting their careers. The perfect demonstration of Doris Day's Hollywood status was the fact that *Lucky Me* proved she too was one of that select band.

But she didn't know it at the time. In fact, she was so disturbed at being associated with such a cine-turkey that she took to her bed the moment it was finished. No one said so at the time, but she was in the midst of a nervous breakdown.

It was all, she would write, 'a hideous nightmare'. That the one with the reputation for being the most stable woman in Hollywood should have been so affected was stunning news – and news that Marty did his best to scotch. He called a press conference with the aim of showing that there was nothing wrong with his wife, certainly nothing that would interfere with her fast-track career prospects. But there were worries aplenty for her. A lump under her left breast made her worry about cancer. The fears turned out to be unfounded – the lump was benign – but the shock remained.

Plainly, she was ill – physically or psychosomatically, it didn't really matter. There were heart palpitations and breathing difficulties. She was hyperventilating. A specialist recommended a daily swim, not difficult for a Hollywood star, and it seemed to have the desired effect.

But it didn't shelter her from the anxiety that followed a threatened kidnapping. A series of obscene phone calls – she was so unnerved by them that she refused to answer the phone unless she could be sure it was Marty at the other end – was followed by a letter threatening to kidnap Terry. The fear remained for weeks, all the time, in fact, that there was a police guard on her home – until an ex-convict was found bleeding to death with sticks of dynamite strapped to him. That was when it was finally revealed that the man had been trying to extort money from her.

There were others who were now saying that Doris herself was trying to extort – not money, of course, but support from her fans without offering enough in return. The night that 'Secret Love' won its Academy Award, Warner Bros hoped that Doris would be there to sing the winning song. She wasn't. Members of the Academy of Motion Picture Arts and Sciences were pretty disappointed, too. They suggested that she was biting the hand that had fed her so generously – a kind of sulk resulting from the fact that she hadn't won an Oscar herself. (Even worse, she hadn't been nominated.)

It was probably just another symptom of her problems. An additional problem, however, was the remarkably unfriendly press she was now getting. Journalists revelled in stories that she was mismanaging her finances – an issue that would recur a decade or so later to an incredible degree. When a newspaperman discovered that for weeks she had left a cheque for $5,000 (a huge amount forty-five years ago) under a pile of fan mail without wondering where it had gone, it didn't do a great deal for her public reputation.

There were compensations, though. She was becoming more and more a follower of Christian Science and it offered her comfort when nothing else seemed to be able to do that. Unusually, she didn't eschew conventional medical help – at least in emergencies. There was a Christian Science 'practitioner' in whom she had total faith, but ultimately, when she felt she was on the verge of a heart attack, she called a doctor. She went into hospital, continued to read *Science and Health* and, before long, she was better, but it was an experience she wouldn't have wanted to repeat – with or without her faith in Christian Science.

Gunslinger Doris in action in *Calamity Jane*

Eventually, her doctors put her illness down to exhaustion from all the work she had done. Looking at the number of films she had turned out in a handful of years, the records she had pressed and the effects of her not so romantic attachments, each one more stressful than the one before, it was hardly surprising.

If it actually was conventional medicine that brought her back to good health, it didn't stop Christian Science becoming more and more part of her life. As she said, she never prayed. All she ever had to do was 'realize' God.

Doris's great success has always been that people 'realized' her and the importance she played in the movie business – to some of them, the importance she played in their own lives. Remember, she herself liked to say that she didn't consider herself to be a star. It wasn't true. No star could achieve that role without believing in herself, and clearly she did. She was also well aware of the problems of stardom and it could be safely assumed that she didn't like those. A star's life was, she said, a 'goldfish bowl'.

The *Lucky Me* team: Doris, Phil ('Bilko') Silvers, Nancy Walker and Eddie Foy, Jr

The fact that in the centre of that goldfish bowl was her own private life didn't help either her health or her attitudes to the way that life was practised one little bit.

Miraculously, she had managed to keep out of the press some of the things that were happening to her marriage. The woman who plainly enjoyed the physical side of marriage (she was to say that the greatest thing about her brief second marriage – and even after the marriage had ended – was how she enjoyed sleeping with George Weidler) was having problems. Problems, it was said by close intimates, with her sexual relationship with Melcher. She wasn't sure either that he was looking after her career as caringly as he had in the past. What she didn't know was that he was also manipulating her financial affairs as though he was standing over an open drain.

That wouldn't appear obvious until later on, but, for whatever reason, they had a trial separation. It seemed that, whatever she did to try to make things work out, Doris Day and marriage didn't go together like a horse and carriage. She might have been content with allowing yet another husband to take a trip to the divorce court, but Melcher wasn't like the others. He wouldn't just lie down and let it happen to him. He begged her to agree to give their relationship another try. She agreed – and as far as the public was concerned, all was well with them again.

Her next movie seemed to demonstrate the fact that, private life apart, he was advising her well enough in her career. It was to be her last picture under her Warner Bros contract, a swan-song that would be worth singing.

Nobody would describe *Young at Heart* as a great film. But the word 'heart' was written all over it. The fact that it also starred Frank Sinatra didn't do the whole any harm. Sinatra was at the zenith of his comeback career, just a year after *From Here to Eternity*. He acted superbly, conveying every inch of the agony his character's inferiority complex betrayed. His singing on film – particularly of the title number behind the credits – was never better. But he brought a number of problems in his wake – he insisted on a new ending for the film (he refused to die), he didn't like the cameraman, Charles Lang (whom he demanded be replaced), and he wouldn't work if Marty Melcher was around. As Doris was discovering, there were a lot of people who felt much the same about her husband.

Love Me
or Leave Me

Young at Heart wasn't exactly the way that Doris felt. The strains were tremendous. She didn't care much for Sinatra. But she was proving to be so professional, you would never have known about any of those problems.

And the part suited her like a couturier's new dress. She was playing another of those roles at which she would become expert – the beautiful daughter, wise beyond her years, who shows that she can leave her rose-covered home and survive in abject poverty without losing either her beauty or her dignity, even when her girl-next-door clothes are replaced by suitably dowdy outfits.

What is more, she picks up a sheet of music just handed to her by Sinatra the songwriter and warbles his tunes like 'You, My Love' as though she had been singing them all her life, although the big hit of the film was 'Ready, Willing and Able'.

This was a remake of *Four Daughters*, the 1938 film that had starred Priscilla Lane as well as John Garfield in his first role. It was also written by the same people, Julius Epstein and Lenore Coffee.

'It was a happy film the second time,' Epstein told me. Unlike the first picture, this one had only three daughters. It was also in colour and, of course, it had the music – an entirely suitable addition to this story of the daughters of a music teacher in one of those warm, homespun small towns so beloved of Hollywood at the time.

Instead of a fourth daughter, there was the towering presence of Ethel Barrymore as the father's sister. The other girls were played by Dorothy Malone (trying to look sultry) and Elizabeth Fraser (succeeding in looking plump and homely). Each one of the girls had boyfriends who brought their own troubles – the main one being no one could be sure who was going to end up with whom. There were road crashes, hospital beds and drunks. But it was that homespun heart that made it work. Perhaps Doris suffered by being overshadowed by Sinatra, who was undoubtedly the star of the piece, but

76

Rehearsing with Frank Sinatra for *Young at Heart*

Doris shines through in *Young at Heart*, with an anxious-looking Sinatra

anyone wanting to see her at her best as both an actress and a velvet-smooth singer just had to see her in this.

It was a film that no Doris Day fan could consider omitting from their 'collection' of her movies that they had seen. Neither could they have missed *Love Me or Leave Me*, another movie set in the 1920s. But it was as different from her other jazz age films as it would be possible to imagine. No happy love story there – and certainly no humour.

For this, the top musical star of the 1950s had moved to the greatest musical factory of them all – MGM.

We saw a Doris Day who still looked lovely, wearing clothes more accurate for the period than ever before, and singing more powerfully than in the past.

Actually, power is what this picture represents. James Cagney was her co-star, a presence never easy to compete with. Yet this time it is Doris Day's film – a star, slapped and beaten by a man who might just have had a heart of gold beneath his seemingly wicked exterior, but it took a lot to believe it. Marty the Gimp, the Cagney gangster character, limped his way through the movie, slapping and shooting in the process.

Yes, eventually, you did feel sorry for him, but it took a little effort to accept how he browbeat Doris Day into marrying him. She was Ruth Etting, the 1920s singing star who introduced 'Love Me or Leave Me' itself, as well as 'Ten Cents a Dance' – a song that Doris sings to illustrate the way she makes her living. They called them taxi dancers in those days; in other words, dancers for hire.

It was a brave move on her part – and no doubt on Melcher's, too. Tremendous risks were involved in converting the Day personality to that of a woman who – the movie was made in the 1950s, so the script only hinted at the fact – sold more than just dances before making it big as a jazz-age songstress.

Doris said she had plenty of doubts herself. The violence worried her. So did something else – 'there is a scene in which I had to appear in my slip and Cagney is in the room. I was shy about that. I'm a modest person.' It shows how long ago 1954 was. She said she was even reluctant to see the picture because of that scene 'and I don't think I will for years. I certainly won't let my son Terry see it – ever.'

But then you have to realize that the words Ruth Etting and morals didn't exactly go together easily. Certainly, the names Doris Day and Ruth Etting didn't combine all that obviously either. The fans weren't at all sure. For months, she was overwhelmed with letters from people who loved the Doris they knew. They didn't know what had hit them. But they still loved her songs, like 'I'll Never Stop Loving You' which was fairly standard Doris Day material.

Accepting the less usual Day output, you could say, was a marvellous tribute to an actress who had taken her work so seriously. To convince people that she was something that she so manifestly was not was a triumph for any performer. But it wasn't as simple as that. She said that she felt as though she actually were Ruth Etting.

Even worse, every time she and 'the Gimp' had one of their rough and tumble scenes, she pictured not Marty Snyder in front of her, but Marty Melcher. The irony in the similarity of their names was not something she could overlook that easily.

But she tried, although their marriage seemed to be on the rocks for the same sort of reasons as those experienced by Snyder and Etting in the film. People working on the movie didn't exactly find Mr Melcher – or 'Mr Day' as some, to his utter distaste, were beginning to call him – pleasant company. He ranted, he shouted – and he liked to prove he knew everything there was to be known about films and about music. The principal characteristic about 'The Gimp' was that he bossed his wife and her producers in equal measure, deciding how he wanted her work to be projected. What was more, Snyder knew no more about show business than did Melcher.

But that was never the case with Doris, who knew her own business through and through. In *Love Me or Leave Me*, Doris herself had never been better – even if most of the newspaper space was reserved for James Cagney playing a tough guy once more, even one with a limp.

She prepared for the film by listening to everything that the real Ruth Etting ever recorded – not, as she said in her autobiography, to mimic her, but to get the feel of what she did. She didn't, necessarily, study Marty the Gimp that closely. If she had, she might have known that he would attack her mercilessly. Cagney, an actor who used the Method before the Method was invented, did just that – attacked her mercilessly, ripping her dress and doing all sorts of things to her that were strictly *verboten* in a Hollywood still owing allegiance to the Hays Code.

Compared with the violence exhibited, the sight of Doris Day in her slip was suitable for children's Saturday morning cinema shows.

She seems to have been shocked by Cagney's interpretation of what he believed the Gimp would have done. But, as things were, she was even more shocked by what the censors did to the final picture. You might, seeing the film now, think that the gangster was pretty tough with her. It was nothing compared with the sort of material left on the cutting-room floor.

But it did nothing to modify her admiration for an actor who was dominating Warner Bros long before she ever dreamed of facing a movie camera.

I once asked Cagney what he thought of Doris Day (I was working on a BBC radio programme on his life, which then became a biography of the star). 'Guileless,' he said, 'a wonderful actress who gave all of herself to what she did. Next to *Yankee Doodle Dandy*, it was my favourite film – largely because of her. I know I went too far in that. When I slapped her, I actually hit her on the face – so hard that she almost cried. You could see the tears in her eyes. She understood why I did it – and I understood that only a really great actress would accept it. In her case, it really did bring out the brilliance in her.'

If Doris had previously been sold on the basis of being the girl next door, after seeing that film you wondered if you'd even want to live that close to her.

As a career move, making the picture turned out to be a brilliant decision. It was just the right combination for her, with virtually equal opportunities to show off both her acting and singing talents. Needless to say, the title song became a big hit, played on radio shows on both sides of the Atlantic until people got fed up with what was almost the tongue-twisting lyric. The best tribute to her was to say that she sounded better singing the Etting tunes than Ms Etting ever did herself.

Marty Melcher rejoiced. When they arrived for the première of the film, it seemed that they were rejoicing in each other. But it was a front. The marvellous score of *Love*

Sparkling as a 'taxi dancer' in *Love Me or Leave Me*

Me or Leave Me wouldn't have featured in the usual kind of picture that Marty chose for his wife. She disliked the way he tried to save money on her movies, turning them from a quality product into no more than what he believed her public wanted to see.

For instance, she wanted Henry Mancini to do the music for her films. Melcher always found someone cheaper. The result was that there were few hit records to go along with those pictures that used the also-ran composers.

That, of course, wouldn't be the problem with *Love Me or Leave Me*. MGM would never have made it with either an inferior score or poor musicians to play it.

Her professional – as well as much about her private – relationship with Melcher was such a disappointment to Doris. Marty had seemed like a good choice for a husband at first. He was caring and they appeared to get on well together. But little of that was left by the time *Love Me or Leave Me* finished filming. The title had almost got to the stage of being an ultimatum in their marriage.

True, she had always been grateful for the way he had adopted Terry, giving him a home as well as a name. But now she wasn't at all happy with the way he was carrying out his fatherly duties. In fact, Doris's mother, Alma, says she saw him grab the boy so hard, she thought he had broken Terry's arm. His influence was strong. Marty sent his stepson to military school – an institution to which he was as unsuited as a cat to a duck pond.

James Cagney was a tough proposition for Doris in *Love Me or Leave Me*

But Terry would say that he was sure that his stepfather's problem was that he hadn't achieved anything on his own. Marty depended on Doris, but had none of her talent. Plainly, this was really an immense inferiority complex at work.

Years later, when he heard songs that Terry had written, Melcher offered to publish them in his own company. But then, when the youngster was established as a songwriter, Marty told him to go elsewhere to get his work sold. They agreed that Melcher would pay him all that was owed. When Terry got the cheque – for $345,000 – he tore it up. He wasn't going to allow his stepfather to enjoy the fact that he had done so much for the younger man without making a penny. He said that the cash would be payment for all the years of board and lodging that Melcher had given him.

Nevertheless, Terry, who later became an important record producer, agreed that there were plenty of times when his mother and stepfather seemed to get on well. He made her laugh and for someone with as complex a life as Doris – to say nothing of all that had gone on in her life before then – a sense of humour was important.

What was even more worrying was how Doris disliked Marty's inferiority complex. She also hated the way that he assuaged his conscience by taking her money and running to whatever 'investment' he had in mind, like a hotel which she considered to be the epitome of bad taste.

Meanwhile, he and his lawyer-business partner, Jerome Rosenthal were making other investments she knew nothing about. There were oil wells. Oil couldn't go wrong. Could it?

When Doris was introduced to Rosenthal, she didn't like him much. But she could have no idea how big a part he would play in her life.

Then there was the way Marty treated her brother Paul, an epileptic who had come to work for Melcher's production company. It was only after Paul died that she realized that her husband had not been paying him a salary he could live on – not paying it with Doris's money, that is.

People say now that no one liked Marty Melcher. That could be with the benefit of hindsight, but I have to say I have not unearthed any evidence to show that he was a gift to humanity. When she wrote her book, Doris called as many people as possible to give evidence about her husband and about the way he behaved towards her.

James Garner said that he couldn't possibly like Melcher – because he himself was so fond of Doris.

Her friend, Sam Weiss, even attacked Marty's religious beliefs. 'Mr Day' – the inevitable way he would be addressed at the time – had given up his Judaism when he married Doris. Then he followed her in becoming a Christian Scientist. He only did that, said Weiss, because he wanted to impress his wife.

He didn't exactly impress her when Weiss disclosed he had been used as a 'beard' by Melcher – a front for when he was having dates with other women.

Now other questions were being incubated. Why was Melcher making so many trips – on his own – to Europe? Was there really another woman? People would wonder whether, because he wasn't taking Doris with him on holiday, he was consoling himself by just taking her money on a trip – perhaps to a numbered Swiss bank account. If he did, it was never discovered.

But Doris herself agreed later that at the time they had fun – they went to baseball games together, joining other Hollywood celebrities at a local ballpark.

And, it has to be said, she would later admit that it took a long time before she suspected he was anything but honest in the running of her business affairs. At the time, she was saying that all was well with her marriage – or at least with the kind of marriage she decided she would now have.

She didn't even, she would say in her autobiography, miss sex. Newspapers (which were making suggestions that she and the physical side of life were important companions now) printed stories that made her, as she said, the 'Lady Bountiful of the Sheets'. She retaliated by saying that she had no interest in sex when there wasn't a man around whom she loved. Naturally enough, she despised the merest hint of her being something like Hollywood's number one nymphomaniac.

But she wondered about her image – the change from virgin to Lady Bountiful – especially when the producer Herbert Ross started calling her a 'wild ass': 'I'm just the old-fashioned peanut-butter girl next door and you know it,' she retorted. Which was plainly just what she was not. Sex was vitally important to her. And she could even turn the professional virgin tag to her own advantage. 'When men call you that, it usually means you won't sleep with them. I'm happy to be regarded as strong enough to resist all that. I'm also flattered – it sounds as if they want to.'

Whatever else it was that she and her husband had together, allowing him to enjoy her sexual appetite was not going to be one of them – and it seems clear that she didn't allow anyone else to do so either.

There were rumours about just who was getting beneath those sheets with her. Among them was Jimmy Hoffa, the union leader who was later rumoured to have been buried beneath the cement foundations of a bridge – without going through the formality of dying first. She hadn't even met him.

The other suggested lover really got people's attention. A supermarket tabloid ran a massive feature saying that she and Frank Sinatra were more than just good friends. In fact, they weren't even bad friends. They weren't friends at all. She had worked with him in *Young at Heart*, didn't terribly enjoy the experience, and that was it.

Doris knew what the papers were saying and for a period it seemed as if it was only a matter of time before she and Marty Melcher would divorce. But they stayed together, even though she continued to hate much about him.

And she also remained faithful. In a later film, *Where Were You When the Lights Went Out?*, one of the male characters says that he would have loved to have had an affair with her – and even if there had been one, it wouldn't have mattered just so long as her husband never found out.

'But in real life I know I'd never forgive myself if that happened,' she said. 'Call that Yankee-Doodle-Dandy, middle-class morality, but that's the way I feel. The square, corn- tassel dialogue. Right?'

But Marty remained her principal business adviser. What he said, went. How adroit he was in selecting his wife's material will always be a matter for conjecture. Was she wise in accepting the entreaties of one of the great figures in Hollywood history, or should she have resisted him? It all hinged on her husband.

The Man Who Knew Too Much, made in 1956, was the first of the contemporary

Doris and Marty Melcher enjoying a baseball game

Naïve no longer – the newly sophisticated Doris in *The Man Who Knew Too Much*, with James Stewart

movies in which the girl who had always been made to look as if she could as easily switch her hairstyle to pigtails as paint freckles over her face, was now the adult, sophisticated woman who wore those beautifully tailored suits that sent other females into drools of envy.

She wouldn't admit to that persona in real life. 'When everything is so terribly sophisticated,' she would say, 'it's a bore, a fraud. I like that naïve quality.'

Maybe that was what really singled out the type of person she played. A sophisticate, but a naïve one at that. A contradiction? Not the way Doris Day played her.

The Man Who Knew Too Much was essentially another straight role, but it did give her a chance to sing 'Que Sera Sera' for the first time – which meant a chance to establish for herself yet another trademark. The record of the song sold three million copies.

There would never be a bigger Doris Day hit.

Of course, she said that *que sera sera* had always been her own philosophy – even before the song was written. That was the one undoubted success about this movie – the kind of hit record virtually any other singer would die for. The film itself also gave her an opportunity to play opposite James Stewart. Most significantly of all, it meant she was working for Alfred Hitchcock.

'Hitch' had made *The Man Who Knew Too Much* before – and a lot more successfully – in 1934. But now, all those years later, it is interesting enough to see it as a chance for Doris Day to blossom in what was for her an unconventional role. It was a challenge to which she rose out of all proportion to the resultant movie. In the film, she played the mother of a kidnapped boy and the wife of a rather bored looking Mr Stewart. But this was one of the first movies in which it was enough just to watch Doris and then soak up the colour of Morocco, where the early part of the movie was filmed.

It wasn't an easy picture to make. And, truth to tell, Doris Day, now the big star, was behaving like the big star – or perhaps that should be THE Big Star.

She complained about having to go abroad to make the movie – to London and to Marrakesh. Doris didn't want to fly, which was the reason, she said in her own book, why she had never gone abroad with Bob Hope. But Hitchcock wanted her and he was filming abroad, like it or not.

She didn't even like 'Que Sera Sera'.

She liked London, but hated Marrakesh. It was the first demonstration of Doris Day, the animal lover, coming into conflict with Doris Day, the actress. The animals she was supposed to have in her film were emaciated and, she believed, badly treated. So she refused to perform until they were fed properly. If Mr Hitchcock didn't like what she did, she said, he could get Grace Kelly.

That didn't exactly endear her to Hitch. But then she wasn't much impressed by Hitch. She complained time after time to anyone who would listen that she knew he didn't like her. Well, he was entitled to his view. But he wasn't entitled to ignore her, which she thought very rude.

In later years, she was told how lucky she was. Hitch had a reputation as a man whose hands became very busy when in close contact with one of his seemingly ice-cold blonde maidens in their tight-fitting suits and dresses. 'He behaved himself (in that respect),' she would say. 'Oh, yes. He behaved himself.'

Whether he would have behaved himself if Marty hadn't been around every moment is another matter. Others say that was Doris's big problem. With no Melcher controlling all her movements, she might have become a great character actress.

Eventually, she braved Hitchcock's lair herself. He said that he hadn't communicated with her simply because he had no complaints with what she did.

That took a little stretch of the imagination to get through, but it did. Her relationship with her co-star was less fraught.

James Stewart once told me for a BBC interview: 'I loved working with Doris. She was very much a star, but always denied that she was.' Or rather, perhaps, pretended to deny that she was.

Julie, later that year, was another straight role and another one with a sinister theme – the attempt by a concert pianist to murder his wife. What was going on now? That charming girl next door was specializing in playing women victims, women who suffered. In this picture, co-starring Louis Jourdan, she was also a woman who was depended upon to do the impossible – like piloting an aircraft to safety when she didn't know the difference between a joystick and an altimeter. There were similarities between this and any one of the movies in the *Airport* series, but you had to ask yourself what Doris Day was doing in a disaster movie – apart from risking making a disaster of her career.

She had to ask herself the same question – and frequently did. She hated the script and complained about it to Marty time after time. Time after time, that is, that she said she hadn't been consulted about making it before her husband signed the contract.

Marty, for his part, insisted time after time that he knew what was right for her. What may not have been so obvious then was that he had a role for himself in the picture – as producer. He was no longer going to be just co-producer. Doris worried about that – and with good reason.

Now, you have to realize that this was the woman who was frightened to fly in a normal passenger aircraft and was now not only having to act out the possibility of saving a crashing plane, but to take flying lessons.

She wasn't actually expected to take off, but she was expected to handle the controls and make it look as though it was the most natural thing in the world.

She actually did crash during the filming – and for real. But it was her Cadillac that was smashed to smithereens when hit broadside on by a driver who had run through a red light. She had medical attention and was pronounced shaken but not hurt.

It wasn't the only time in the production that she and hospitals came face to face with each other. She was suffering from extreme pain towards the end. That and excessive vaginal bleeding. Once the shoot was over and she was back home, her gynaecologist diagnosed a huge tumour. It wasn't malignant, but her intestines were

On the set of *The Man Who Knew Too Much*, **with Hitchcock and James Stewart**

damaged and she had to have a hysterectomy. It was not the first time that the Christian Science to which she remained devoted had failed to come up with a solution to her health problems.

It wasn't good news for her. Secretly, she had looked forward to having a new baby – she thought that Marty would make a great father, and that a baby could have

WHAT HAPPENED TO JULIE ON HER HONEYMOON?

M·G·M PRESENTS

DORIS DAY
LOUIS JOURDAN
BARRY SULLIVAN
FRANK LOVEJOY

IN

JULIE

AN ARWIN PRODUCTION

WRITTEN AND DIRECTED BY ANDREW L. STONE
PRODUCED BY MARTIN MELCHER

A METRO GOLDWYN MAYER RELEASE

RUN JULIE RUN, RUN FOR YOUR LIFE!

cemented their marriage. She felt that she would be able to spend more time with a new baby than she had ever managed with Terry, a boy she had barely known, and who had been brought up by his grandmother.

It seemed as though the old Doris Day glory days were over. But she was lucky. The magic touch didn't elude her. In 1957 she made *The Pajama Game*, one of the most joyous experiences of all her appearances on screen.

Doris apparently didn't find the experience particularly joyous herself, though. In her autobiography, she dismisses it in one sentence and says that it was 'arduous' because she was the only one in the cast who hadn't been in the Broadway show. That comment plainly hides a great deal of resentment. Was she badly treated by the other members of the cast? They seem to have resented her presence and to have conveyed that resentment to her.

The triumph was that people sitting in cinema audiences weren't aware of any bad feeling – which means there must have been some pretty good acting and singing involved.

The Pajama Game had been a hit Broadway musical in an age of hit Broadway musicals. It was of the same generation as *Guys and Dolls*, *The King and I* and *My Fair*

Lady. Improbably, the notion of a strike in a pyjama, no, pajama (even the British production used the American spelling) factory, made a terrific show. It was a tightly written story with a lot of humour and some great songs. In the movie version, Doris Day just served to make it all look and sound even better. 'Hey There', 'Once a Year Day', 'Hernando's Hideaway' and the title song were made to measure for an age that seemed to be on the cusp of an economic security never known before.

In England, the Prime Minister, Harold Macmillan, told people they had never had it so good and men and women on both sides of the Atlantic were ready to believe it. When Doris sang the *Pajama Game* tunes, audiences were prepared to dance out of the theatre humming them on their way to the brand new cars and motor scooters that would take them to their comfy new homes.

When people got to those homes and turned on their radios, Doris could still be heard singing 'Que Sera Sera'. Now, though, when they heard the song, they thought they knew the answer to their own questions about security in the years to come – Doris Day singing to them was an omen that said whatever would be, would be – good. But she wasn't going to be the same Doris people knew and loved.

That Touch of Mink

She continued to worry about the films she made. 'Sure there were roles I would have loved to have played and I know my husband blocked them,' she would say. On the other hand, she had a lot to be thankful for.

It was *The Man Who Knew Too Much* that should have convinced her. People liked the feisty woman in the smart clothes that made her look sexy in a different kind of way from the usual Hollywood stereotype. She never revealed too much, or even a suggestion of too much, but she was a walking fashion plate of the kind that made women want to wear the clothes she wore and men dare to wonder what was underneath it all. Oscar Levant's virgin was clearly not that any more. Julie Andrews had taken over the role and Doris was pleased to give it to her.

What was even more significant about the Hitchcock movie was the subtle way the song 'Que Sera Sera' was placed in the action. Doris Day had found a way of singing in a non-musical picture. From now on, with the very odd exception, that would be the way things were to go. Truthfully, this was a new era. No longer tied to Warner's apron strings, she was making movies as different from the Doris Day classics as it was possible for them to be. It wouldn't be unkind to say that they were all of a formula, but it was one that audiences wanted. She was also heading what was now a Doris Day repertory company – time and again appearing with the kind of young (but not too young), sophisticated, well-dressed handsome men who were considered right for her image: Rock Hudson, a man who called her Eunice and with whom she had a very pleasant relationship before anyone doubted his macho sexuality; Gig Young, before he grew into his later lean, hungry, haggard look; and James Garner: all suited the position of the men who chased Doris before she caught them.

And that was the point of the series, which went on and on, just as the queues to buy tickets for them went on and on.

With Clark Gable in *Teacher's Pet* – one of the big films of 1957

She was the attractive businesswoman/housewife/teacher who became involved in situations never of her own making – mistaken intentions or identities, usually ones that made her fall in love with the dastardly hero, only to discover that he wasn't such a hero after all, before realizing that she had made a terrible mistake and that he was really very nice indeed. That, needless to say, was enough to get them into a final clinch and for Doris to sing the title song or some other appropriate ditty over the titles, a nice ruse that, since it kept customers in the theatre until it was time for the lights to go up.

The plots were interchangeable – and so were the sets and the costumes. Whether they were made for MGM, Universal or Paramount, they all looked alike. Invariably, she lived in the same kind of house, was driven to the same kind of executive office in the same kind of large, expensive car. The exasperated Doris Day sigh (more of a sexy grunt) became as familiar as the Doris Day voice once had been.

But whatever the similarities, and no matter the details of the story, most of them had a uniform charm. Just as in the very earliest days (and it had all really been happening in less than a decade), there was a trademark about them and people knew what they were getting. The logo had been updated, but she was offering a discernible

**Steve Forrest (at left) with Doris the lobster lady and
Jack Lemmon in *It Happened to Jane***

product that you either liked or rejected. On balance, more people liked than rejected them. The first in the series was one of the best known. *Teacher's Pet* didn't confine itself to members of the repertory company. Clark Gable had always been out there on his own and he had long left behind any suggestion that he could be part of a team. This wasn't the old Gable lover type either. Now he was the crusty newspaperman who falls for a night-school teacher and enrols as her pupil. It was the classic plot that we would soon come to recognize. Doris takes a man at his word and fumes when she discovers she has been deceived. Gig Young was on hand to complicate matters – and Doris was available to sing the title song. She was also available to be under Gable's spell. She admired his masculinity, his failure to give the impression of being not just the King, but the Emperor of Hollywood. There were no big retinues for him, just a make-up man and a stand-in with whom he would share a nip of whisky and then go home to his wife. But above all, she relished his lack of complication. If only Marty...

That wasn't worth thinking about. But her relationship with Gable was enough to make *Teacher's Pet* one of the big films of 1957.

The next year, there was *The Tunnel of Love*. Now it was Richard Widmark in the Gable role (this time as a man trying to adopt an orphan, who wonders if in an unguarded moment he should have seduced the agency official arranging the deal – Doris, of course) and again with Gig Young backing up the rear.

It didn't work. But Doris tried. How she tried! During the making of the picture, she banged her head on a post. She was almost knocked unconscious and there was a huge gash on her forehead (which fortunately did not scar sufficiently for it to be noticed) but she insisted carrying on just the same.

It Happened to Jane didn't work either. One might have hoped that the name 'Jane' would have a degree of luck attached to it. But this was no *Calamity Jane*. The director Richard Quine told me: 'This was going to be a chance to make a landmark film. We tried, but it just didn't work out. But it was very popular and I know that I liked it.'

A young Jack Lemmon was there to deal with the farcical situation of Doris playing a lobster saleswoman (well, they had to try to make plots different). No Gig Young in sight this time, although Ernie Kovacs and Steve Forrest were around.

It Happened to Jane did have a certain charm. Jack Lemmon would say that it failed because it had a terrible title. It was simpler than that – people didn't like the sophisticated, beautifully dressed Doris Day looking as though she smelled of fish. As for her selling lobsters – it was another problem that Doris could direct towards her husband.

It convinced Lemmon, one of the most respected actors in Hollywood even then, that Doris was a fellow professional, a compliment that was not to be taken lightly. He would say that she was a Method actor who might or might not have known what it meant. I think that was asking too much of her. She was much more a natural actress than one who had to think too closely about what she did. It is difficult to imagine her telling herself that she was a lobster saleswoman. Even more difficult to imagine that she might go and see actual lobster saleswomen at work – or wear their smelly clothes. A Method actor would have done that – and appeared much less charming than Doris proved herself to be.

But there were achievements – not least in her record career. 'Everybody Loves a Lover' – full of echo chambers and a duet with herself – soared up the charts and won an Emmy award for best vocal performance of 1958.

The classic example of the new Day movie genre was *Pillow Talk* – the first of only three movies with Rock Hudson, but they got on so well that, looking back now, it seems as though they were constantly together on the screen. It would always be her favourite movie of the series. The film was originally to be called *The Way the Wind Blows*, but the producer, Ross Hunter, wanted it to share the name of the song he knew would be a hit. And that was important, not merely because every producer wants

In *Pillow Talk*, the first of her three movies with Rock Hudson

every one of his movies to be big at the box-office, but because he imagined he was in the midst of creating the best comedy pair since William Powell and Myrna Loy made their *Thin Man* series.

What he subsequently would be less keen on sharing was the status of producer – with Marty Melcher. He didn't object so much to the title being shared, but the fact that 'Mr Day' also wanted a $50,000 fee tended to stick in his craw. But he said nothing. It was just another part of the budget and, since he wanted Doris as his star, there didn't appear to be much he could do about it.

He was right about wanting Doris. He was also right about the film. Doris had never met Rock Hudson before and they got on like a soundstage on fire. She didn't know that he had been enchanted by her ever since he first heard her singing 'Sentimental Journey' when he was making unsentimental voyages as a sailor. That was a great story for the publicists – but it only worked until Hudson 'came out'. One needn't doubt, however, his conclusion that there was great chemistry between them. Without it, the series would never have worked. She was once asked how much of the sophisticated woman in those comedies – and the title songs that she sang – were really her. 'They're a part of me,' she answered.

Smart and sexy in *Pillow Talk*

It was another part of her that knew what her public wanted. And one that recognized the chemistry when it worked. Actually, there had to be that chemistry for one of the most deceptive film tricks to work as well as it did in *Pillow Talk*. It doesn't quite rank with the floor over which Harold Lloyd hung from the hands of the skyscraper clock or with the revolving set that made Fred Astaire look as though he was dancing on the ceiling. But when Rock Hudson seemed to be carrying Doris Day out of an apartment building lobby, she was actually resting on a shelf supported from above by invisible wires. As Rock – perhaps an inappropriate name in the circumstances – pointed out, he would have done it easily in just one take, but there were too many takes for him to be able to carry such a sexy, tall woman over and over again. No one complained – and, as far as we know, no one reported seeing the wires.

As for Doris, she loved everything about it – not least because she no longer had to wear smelly clothes. In fact, her wardrobe was created by one of the great fashion names in Hollywood, Jean Louis, and she loved every suit, every hat, every elegant dress that he designed for her.

It was Ross Hunter's idea to put the stress on her clothes. He was voicing what few had done before – the fact that, dressed properly (and, unusually, not undressed), Doris was an extraordinarily sexy woman. It proved to be just about the most successful movie Hunter ever made. The film took off instantly.

It was made to the usual formula, but done better than it had been before or would be again. It had to be done well to survive the basic story line – two people, sharing a party telephone line, hate the sound of each other, but without realizing who the other

Cuddling up to David Niven in the forgettable *Please Don't Eat the Daisies*

is fall in love when they meet. When they do discover each other's real identity, all hell is let loose. Well, of course it is. And of course they make up, and, of course, Doris sings the title song in the background. That was how it always was – after three movies in just over a year – and nobody seemed sorry it was so.

But it wouldn't be quite the same. Doris won an Oscar nomination – but not the Academy Award itself – for *Pillow Talk*. That wouldn't happen again, but the formula was well established and audiences would be the better for it. She was a woman of the 1950s playing a part set in the 1950s made in the 1950s, and that was what people wanted to see.

It was a fact proved by the statistics. Before *Pillow Talk*, she had slipped from her accustomed position of being in the list of top ten film stars. After it, she was number one – a status she retained for the next five years. Considering some of the pictures she would make, that was quite an achievement, but whatever she filmed men and women came to see. So did their children, because parents believed that she was too wholesome to corrupt them.

That was why the formula was something to be repeated time after time. It was

Putting a brave face on *Midnight Lace*, with Rex Harrison

virtually written into her contracts now, and she was pleased to know about it.

Please Don't Eat the Daisies was more of the same – this time with David Niven playing opposite her in the story of a drama critic's family moving to the country. That might have been a good destination for the movie, too, come to think of it.

Midnight Lace was a brief hiatus in the comedy saga. It was also produced by Ross Hunter, who seemed to undo all the love, affection and appreciation that Doris had had for him after *Pillow Talk*.

Doris Day aficionados loved it, but you had to be really committed to say very much about a film set in London in the fog – at which point all serious attention vanished in the mist. There were too many shades of too many better pictures – like *Gaslight* – dealing with a terrorized woman and a husband who might not be all he seems. She looked glamorous enough – when you could see her through the fog, that is.

She was so affected by the film and its plot that she collapsed on the sound stage. But Hunter told her she was magnificent and she found herself suddenly taking on all the feelings that she thought any woman suspecting her husband of something unpleasant would have. When she was about to have her dress torn from her body, the

Doris and Rock again – a happy partnership in *Lover Come Back*

fear and degradation she imagined was much like that which would have been felt by a woman in that position in real life. She liked that dress – made for her by another top Hollywood couturier, Irene, but didn't like it ripped off. It all seemed like a retrograde step. For his part, Rex Harrison, her co-star, always looked as though he would be happier playing Henry Higgins in *My Fair Lady*.

Lover Come Back was more true to form, with her and Rock Hudson involved in an industrial con – they are rival advertising executives engaged in promoting a non-existent product. Which was not what anyone could say about their partnership.

But *Time* magazine was suspicious of what it all meant. Seeing the pair in *Pillow Talk*, said the magazine, had been like watching two shiny new Cadillacs parked side by side. *Lover Come Back* was like seeing two cream puffs (no irony intended, and it wouldn't have been understood at the time if there had been).

Doris generally knew whether movies worked or not. She told *Cosmopolitan* magazine: 'Some of the downbeat pictures, in my opinion, should never [have been] made at all. Most of them are made for personal satisfaction, to impress other actors who go to see the acting, the elements, the naturalness and say, "Oh God! What

With Marty Melcher on the set of *That Touch of Mink*

camerawork!" But the average person in the audience, who bought his ticket to be entertained, doesn't see all that. He comes out depressed. He doesn't feel good or lifted.'

That was what worried film studios. They wanted to be 'lifted' by their stars. They didn't like them speaking their mind and Doris was a gal whose mind was there to be spoken. 'She's not only natural, she's genuine, artless and congenial,' wrote David Shipman in *Picture Show* in September 1952.

The movies were the bedrock of Doris's work. But when she made records they sold well – including an album with André Previn, called 'Duet'. But what fans really wanted were her renditions of numbers like 'A Guy Is a Guy', 'Bewitched' (from the newly revived *Pal Joey*) and 'Everybody Loves a Lover', as well as any theme from her latest movie. When she sang 'If I Give My Heart to You', it was a proposition many a young, well-scrubbed youngster on an American beach party would hope might be put into operation.

That Touch of Mink had a touch of we've-been-here-before about it, but then, that was what people wanted – or studios like United Artists would never have made it. This story of a secretary being chased by her boss, would raise more yawns than laughs today, but in 1962 there were supposedly people around who found it all very shocking. Nevertheless, Grant and Day made a good partnership and Gig Young was there to stamp the trademark on it all.

The only trouble was that title – as far as she was concerned. The woman who would later become an animal-rights activist shudders at the name of the picture and what she wore in it. 'At the time I was not educated about animals and actually wore mink in the film. For that reason alone, I wouldn't watch the film now. Just to think I actually wore mink!' But the mink wasn't the only difficulty. The relationship between Cary and Doris was not exactly one made in heaven. She would complain that they both liked to be photographed from their right profile – an impossible arrangement for a couple on film, unless they spend the whole movie standing in line. But you have to accept that they didn't get on at all and the camera angle was the only thing that either of them wanted to talk about in public. The film wasn't great, although the box-office seemed to indicate that it was good enough – and Doris, as we have seen, kept her place on the Hollywood totem pole. (She also received the critics' Sour Apple and Most Unco-operative Actress Awards; she didn't like giving interviews and didn't want to get involved in too many questions – which may have had something to do with the way she perceived Marty was treating her.)

Variety noted at the time: 'Throughout, the determination is to keep faith with the American sex mythology at all costs.' Well, American sex mythology (and every other kind) has changed more than a little in the last forty years, but see *Mink* on TV and Doris Day still looks terrific. Which is remarkable when you realize what she was going through at the time. As noted, she was a sexy woman – a sexy woman who enjoyed sex. It was not something said very openly at the time, but sex was important to her – much more than it was to her husband, a fact that might amaze the men who gazed longingly at her on screen.

Sexual deprivation and the worries about what she was doing with her career and her investments were all having their effect. Doris and Marty separated. But not for long.

He pleaded with her to take him back. As he said, so many of their investments were in their joint names that a separation could make them both broke. So, for financial reasons, they came back together again – in public. The press loved the huge diamond ring he gave her – she said it had a huge flaw in it, too, but didn't publicize that fact. As far as she was concerned, any real marriage was over. There would be no more sex – a sacrifice on her part, but it was also a fact that she no longer fancied him in bed. It was a financial arrangement. She could not know then that it wouldn't even be that.

On the set of *That Touch of Mink* with Cary Grant

Send Me No Flowers

You have to ask yourself why Doris Day gave up making solid, honest-to-goodness musicals so suddenly. People still liked to hear her records. In 1962, 'Lover Come Back' did extremely well, as different a kind of Doris Day song as her films were different from the kind she had made for Warner Bros not long before.

But musicals? That seemed to be in the past. The answer is that Hollywood had more or less given up on making solid, honest-to-goodness musicals altogether. For reasons no one has adequately been able to explain, they just went out of fashion. With Gene Kelly getting a little too long in the tooth to shout 'Gotta Sing, Gotta Dance', virtually the only musicals being filmed were movie versions of stage shows (like, heavens be thanked, *The Pajama Game*). There were a few specially made musicals, like the fairly appalling Sinatra – Crosby vehicle, *Robin and the Seven Hoods*, but they were so few that you could count them on the fingers of your left hand.

For those movie fans for whom musicals were the great art form of the twentieth century, the one thing that only a movie could do (the stage musical was always a different animal and one of the reasons why Hollywood came unstuck with their all-singing, all-dancing formula was that they failed to realize the fact), that was close to a tragedy.

There had at one time been talk of Doris making the film of *The Sound of Music*. As part of a campaign to get the role, she recorded a number of songs from the show. But the part, as history now records, went to that other former perpetual virgin, Julie Andrews.

The fact that Doris's next movie was to be a new musical is probably the only reason *Jumbo* is worth mentioning at all. A circus story in which Doris co-starred with Jimmy Durante and an elephant, this was one of the worst musicals ever made and one that

With Jimmy Durante and the scene-stealing elephant in the dismal *Jumbo*

could probably cause Ms Day to be persuaded to dip into her chequebook if you promised not to remind her of it. As Leslie Halliwell, author of the famous *Film Guide*, notes: 'the elephant stole the show'. All of which was a great pity – since the film was based on a highly successful Rodgers and Hart musical show written by Ben Hecht and Charles MacArthur, the partnership best known for the newspaper story, *The Front Page*.

It couldn't have been easy to work out what would come next. The modern comedy needed to be done as a series. Having breaks from the formula risked losing its appeal. But it happened and she survived.

The formula came back and Doris was back on form. *The Thrill of It All* in 1963 had her as the wife of a gynaecologist (James Garner) who decides she would rather be a model working on TV commercials. *Move Over Darling*, that same year, was again with Mr Garner – the husband whom she discovers has remarried during the five years

Doris and Stephen Boyd in *Jumbo*

she was away after carelessly being shipwrecked. It was fun and looked marvellous. Also, Doris's record company couldn't have been too disappointed with it. The title song was another of those big Day hits, which these days finds itself on dozens of compilation albums. What was remarkable about the song was that it was written by Doris's son, Terry. What was not remarkable was that the 'Auntie' BBC of the 1950s tried to ban the number because it was considered too suggestive.

And the list continued. *Send Me No Flowers* with Rock Hudson and Tony Randall (who had also been with them in *Pillow Talk* and *Lover Come Back*) deserved more bouquets than it received at the time. In this, she was the wife of a hypochondriac who, thinking he was on his death bed, tries to find her a new husband for when he is no longer around. In 1965 there was *Do Not Disturb* (Rod Taylor's dizzy wife, in London again), which could be seen as a sort of morality play (the message was, only have sex with someone you love).

A year later, came *The Glass Bottom Boat* (with Rod Taylor again; this time, a spy parody, playing a widow). *Caprice* followed in 1967 (co-starring with Richard Harris, now discovering the cosmetics firm for which she works is involved in drug smuggling). 'I never understood that film,' she would say. 'I can't figure it out. I remember that I didn't want to do it. But there was no way out. I had to do it.'

That notion creates a puzzle. Why did she have to do it? Even under contract to a studio, she could have turned down a part and then gone on suspension for the period that the picture was shooting (with the time added to her contract). Even if Marty Melcher was persuading her to do the work, it seems inconceivable that she didn't have the strength to put her foot down and just say no. In so many ways she was a very strong woman indeed. But apparently, she wouldn't do that.

What could make her submit to a man whose credibility she already doubted? One wonders how it was that she allowed her husband to guide her career in any direction without her agreement. History, however, has been full of Svengali and Trilby stories and it seems as though this was the sort of relationship that they had.

That year, 1967, was not the happiest in her life. Her marriage was no better than

Back on form in 1963's *The Thrill of It All*

With James Garner again, for the second time in a year, in *Move Over Darling*

it had ever been. And it was the year when she had to admit defeat. Her big ambition had been to bring her parents together again. But her father had now remarried – the intolerant bigot had found a black bride – so that was not going to be possible. Then, in 1967, Mr Kappelhoff died.

Her next film didn't help her happiness. *The Ballad of Josie* was much worse than most of the movies she had starred in. Now one had to contemplate Doris Day as a sheep farmer in frontierland (selling lobsters became more believable after that). The film was such a flop that it lasted just long enough for the reels to be repacked in their containers and then sent on to the television studios, who showed anything. Then there was *Where Were You When the Lights Went Out?* – the screen adaptation of the story of the night in 1963 when someone pulled the plug on New York's electrical supply.

Doris would say that she didn't like those pictures and the fact that she made them at all was due to her husband.

Was it also because of her husband that she didn't play the part of Mrs Robinson in the 1967 movie *The Graduate*? We will probably never know, although it is interesting to speculate what she might have done with the role that Anne Bancroft

With Rock Hudson again in *Send Me No Flowers*

made all her own, in the film that gave the young Dustin Hoffman his big break. But Doris would only say that she thought it too sexually exploitative.

Could it also have been that she didn't like the idea of being seen to have a son of Dustin Hoffman's age? Her own films never actually crossed the line that would have made them exploitative (*Love Me or Leave Me*, after all, had her as the victim).

And they still did well without the more unpleasant sexual connotations, brought her as much money as fan mail – which she assumed was making her a fortune - and the fans were glad every time they read there would be a new Doris Day movie opening at their neighbourhood cinema.

It seemed never-ending. Doris making light comedies, looking great, always getting the man she wanted, despite all the efforts (not least her own) to thwart it happening. People looked in their newspapers, saw a new Doris Day film advertised called *With Six You Get Egg Roll*, paid their money to see the story of a widow marrying a widower (Brian Keith) and left with the usual, nice, warm feeling inside. What they didn't know was that it was going to be the last Doris Day film they would see – unless she ever decided to make a movie in her old age. It was not a pleasant experience for

Trying to make sense of *Caprice*, with Richard Harris

her. Not because the film was bad. She said she liked the script and the way the filming was going. But there were now other developments in her roller-coaster marriage with Marty Melcher.

For the first time for years, she was telling herself – and other people, too – that she loved him. She was beginning to be convinced that he really had her welfare at heart.

It was 1968 and in the midst of this feel-good time that she began to notice that Marty wasn't his old self. He lost his appetite, he was getting thin, his pallor was turning grey. He grew weaker and weaker, but was refusing medical treatment. Finally, he couldn't fight it any more and was taken to the Mount Sinai hospital. An enlarged heart was diagnosed (which surprised some people who wondered aloud if he had ever had a heart at all). Soon after admission, he died.

It meant a total change to her life – to say nothing of her career. Without Marty there, she could do what she liked. But what did she want to do? The answer was nothing. She wanted to rest. But there were problems. When her financial situation was looked into, her advisers pointed out one remarkable fact. There was no more money

Doris with Brian Keith in 1968's *With Six You Get Eggroll* – the last film she made

– anywhere. In fact, the woman who had made a fortune now owed a fortune. That awakening came in the midst of another decision that Marty had foisted upon her: that was when she realized she wasn't going to make any more films. No. No more films. She was going, instead, to make a TV series. It wasn't just a sudden whim, a change of emphasis in her career like all the others (the band singer who made girl-next-door movies; the nostalgic musicals, the light comedies). This time, she needed the money and she had no choice but to take an offer she could not refuse, even if she had wanted to – and she did.

Storm Warning

There was so much about Doris Day that mystified her fans. They would like to have found that the well-dressed woman they saw on screen, the one who sang like a bird, was for real – and they were discovering day by day that she wasn't. Some were quite shocked to find that she had normal women's feelings. Most of all, they were astonished to read that none of her marriages had had the kind of happy endings that they came to expect from her movies. But it just wasn't like that – at any time.

It was only after Marty Melcher died that Doris Day realized that what she had always thought of as an up-and-down marriage had been as down as it was possible to be.

The woman who thought and hoped against hope that she would finally find happiness the third time around was thwarted again. Marty had not only been difficult to live with, after his death the true extent of his deception was revealed. It was as if he had treated her money as the stake on some giant roulette wheel, blown the lot on the wrong colour and the wrong number and then neglected to tell her about it.

That little detail meant that he had gone through $20 million of her money and another $450,000 besides – the amount that she now owed, mostly in taxes. The hotels and oil wells that she supposedly owned were worthless. There were no cattle on any of the ranches that were supposedly hers. The stock she owned in everything else wasn't worth the paper the certificates were printed on. The royalties from her films were being filched by Marty's lawyer and financial adviser Jerome Rosenthal – who had plainly been advising on how best to give himself his client's wife's money. Later evidence proved that the $20 million had mostly gone the way of Rosenthal, without Melcher being able to do much about it. He trusted his adviser and didn't know how to change things – which may be a charitable way of looking at things. On the other

In her long-running TV series, *The Doris Day Show*

hand, it is amazing that Doris herself didn't see any reason to ask occasionally to look at the books.

What is undeniable is that Doris was left with very much less than nothing as the sum total of seventeen years of marriage and more than two decades of work – with most of the good memories submerged in the bad. Her financial problems, which turned Doris into a one-woman Wall Street Crash, meant that she would have to sell her house and everything else she owned to help pay off her debts.

When Marty died, Doris was in a state of mourning, genuinely missing a man she told herself she had loved deeply. Now that emotion was replaced by severe shock and trauma. That may have been a contributory factor in another change to Doris's lifestyle. She gave up Christian Science. It no longer seemed relevant to her.

Melcher had left Doris with another 'legacy' – *The Doris Day Show*. Doris knew nothing about the television plans until she saw a couple of what she discovered to be preliminary scripts lying around on her late husband's desk. She certainly did not know that CBS had paid a considerable sum in advances and had already spent money on structuring a series that they thought could last five years – without anyone letting the star know that she was involved.

In *The Doris Day Show*, with John Dehner

At the age of forty-four, she was due for another nervous breakdown. This one was different. She did strange, inexplicable things – like walking around in a daze, and, on one horribly memorable occasion, diving into a friend's swimming pool fully clothed.

She wasn't the only 'beneficiary' of the way things had developed. Terry was in a state of shock not much different from that of his mother – and, as executor, he had seen it before she had. His own fortune, as producer of his mother's record albums and other work, had disappeared down the Melcher–Rosenthal drain, too. Ross Hunter wasn't much happier. The commitments he had made to Melcher in the course of agreeing that he should be a joint producer had meant that he was in almost as bad a financial state as she was. He wasn't quite wiped out, but almost. The name Ross Hunter and financial success no longer went hand in hand.

Everyone who knew anything was now blaming Jerome Rosenthal for the folly into which Melcher had (it seemed) himself been led and into which he then led everyone else.

Not least of all the problems that Doris faced was the television series itself –

which she hated. A hatred she demonstrated, she would say, by going through the motions but doing very little about anything, which was one reason why the shows took six days to record instead of the usual four.

She detested the setting. The woman who had been dressed by Jean Louis and Irene, who had looked stunning even in indifferent pictures like *The Tunnel of Love* and *It Happened to Jane*, was sucked into a series in which she appeared as the widow of a farmer, running the farm in his stead – milking cows while looking after a couple of kids and their grandfather.

That wasn't what she wanted out of her show business life. No, the star of *The Man Who Knew Too Much* knew too much herself about the business to be happy with a situation over which she had no control. She, however, was the first to admit the therapeutic properties of having to turn up for work every day and be subject to the controls of the system. In truth, she was lucky to have that sort of work to get on with – even though it prevented her doing any more filming. But it was mediocre stuff and she was the first to admit to it.

Terry wasn't so stuck. He had been appointed executive producer of the series, but he gave up soon after it started.

Doris's son had other problems about this time. For the most innocent of reasons, he became involved with mass murderer Charles Manson. Manson had asked Terry – who was now a respected name in his business and had produced records by The Beach Boys among other top groups – to record some of the songs that he himself had written. (Terry had known Sharon Tate, the actress murdered with Manson's other victims.) When he refused, Manson threatened him – which was why he gave evidence in the murderer's trial and why he needed protection. Soon after the Manson incident, there was another problem – for a time more serious than all the others put together. Terry was involved in a horrific road accident in which his legs were crushed.

Crushed almost as badly as the family fortunes.

You, of course, have to ask yourself how it was that people normally so intelligent and of this world became victims of what was, in effect, a serious confidence trick. No real explanations have ever been offered.

But Jerome Rosenthal was at the bottom of it all, a judge decided. He had creamed commissions from Melcher, made sure that Marty got twenty-five per cent of all that Doris earned, and then took a commission from that money, too. In addition, his unprofessional conduct, said the judge, had resulted in 'phoney' investments. He demonstrated all that by awarding Doris swingeing damages – totalling $22 million.

Doris Day's Best Friends

S o, financially, she was secure again – although in another action, a court agreed she owed the US government $300,000 in income tax. The court found that Melcher (and by association, Doris herself) had engaged in a fraudulent scheme to create transactions that existed only on paper, as a means of evading tax. But it was obvious that she had known nothing about any of it and the $22 million helped to cushion her discomfort.

She made a few records, but before long the appeal of the Doris Day voice on disc waned. She appeared not to let it get her down.

She didn't want to make any more films and no more films came. But she continued with *The Doris Day Show*, this time removed from the farm setting to somewhere more urban and more to her own taste.

The sophisticated Doris Day so beloved of the loyal fans was back. After the first year, she was more fully in control of everything. But even in what she would have said was the dismal farm show, she must have justified its continuation. In a world in which ratings rule everything, hers were strong enough for CBS to want more – and on the evidence of what went out over the ether, the fans did, too. The show lasted for five years – from 1968 to 1973, which was vindication enough.

She also made a series of television commercials for a margarine company – in which she was seen riding a bicycle through the plush streets of Beverly Hills.

She wanted a man in her life. Desperately. But although she fell in love again and for a year had an affair with a married man, whom she never named, it didn't turn into anything. But by then, she had another passion – and one that seemed altogether less complicated. She had always said that she loved dogs as much as people and, one would suspect, probably more so. The statement on the badge she wore on her shoulder, 'I love dogs', surprised no one.

Doris and one of her beloved dogs

Doris posing for the press with Rock Hudson – 'a dear man and I loved him'

It had been a lingering love, ever since that pet dog Tiny died in her arms when she was fifteen. The memory of the time that the little terrier was run over had haunted her and now she never passed a dog walking alone in a busy road without scooping it up in her arms. In the early 1970s, with fewer professional commitments and less financial worry – along with the absence of the kind of romance for which she yearned – she set about doing something about that love of four-legged creatures.

Rescuing a dog injured in a road accident led to helping a stray which she happened upon, one with eye problems. Then there was another injured dog – and another. Before long, she had set up what became the Doris Day Pet Foundation.

Apparently one day she saw a tramp, a dishevelled man, plainly homeless, with a little puppy. She was passing them in her car, did a U-turn and approached the man. She offered him a cheque to give her the dog – so that she could give him a home. The man was reluctant. 'He is my son,' he told her. Eventually, she persuaded him to part with the puppy. The dog – she called him Hobo – had a new home. But the tramp had lost his only companion. It was as if he couldn't argue with her. He took her cheque to the nearest Safeway, told them it came from the famous Doris Day and they cashed it for him.

The income she received as a result of suing Jerome Rosenthal helped her achieve one of the big ambitions in her life – a huge house in an eleven-acre ranch at Carmel in northern California, which would be the centre of her work. Birds and donkeys were looked after along with the dogs and cats. All day long, she was either sorting out the cat litter and cleaning up or cooking the rice and fresh vegetables she thought they needed.

'It has become the most important feature of my life and the most worthwhile,' she told me when I interviewed her about the aims of her Foundation. 'I am dedicated to helping dogs and cats that are strays and which wander the streets near my home.'

She ran a virtual twenty-four-hour dog and cat ambulance service. 'When I get a phone call telling me of an injured pet, I get in my car whatever the time or day to try to rescue it.' She also brought it back to what became both a cat and dog hospital and a pet hotel – in her own home. Cats and dogs had their own beds and she would make sure that each was tucked up warmly and comfortably every night. She had a large van that was converted into a mobile pet's home – with individual cots on a series of vinyl couches that replaced the normal seating.

'I greatly believe that these poor animals have to be given the comfort they deserve,' she said.

With that in mind, she had certain requirements of society. Pet shops should be banned from selling puppies, which she said were not any old commodity. I asked her if she would ever buy a pet from a shop herself. 'Only to get it out of there. There's no place for an animal in a store window.'

And there was one other, even more important priority for her – pet owners should be sure that they neutered or spayed their animals. As she told me: 'It is absolutely essential that that happens. Of course, you could never neuter every animal, but to cut down the agony experienced by strays would be a blessing.' The foundation was there to pay for the spaying of dogs and cats – and then to try to find homes for the animals when they were healthy again.

Before long, the Doris Day Pet Foundation was joined by the Doris Day Animal League, which looks in greater depth at trying to help animals.

Animal lovers around the world made her a virtual saint. They loved the stories of her playing music to her pets (they liked it, she said – just as her plants liked being talked to; they grew better). But she didn't know about that sainthood. After all, she echoed the comment: 'The more I study human beings, the more I like animals.' When someone quoted that back to her, she replied: 'Hear, hear! Well, I do love many, many people. Especially animal people.'

As she said: 'I have vibrations with people who care about dogs. Cats too. Even spiders. I love them. You must learn to love spiders.'

The foundation was founded on the basis, she would explain, that 'there's something about the animals that I just can't do enough for them and I will till the day I die.'

Then, she told me when we met: 'I don't get any applause. I don't want any applause. I use my own money. People do give five dollars, ten dollars. Some people make me cry with their generosity. But we're always on the lookout for some really large donors to get this whole thing going.'

As the years have gone by, 'this whole thing' really has got going.

She was always realistic about the work she was doing. 'I don't think animal abuse will ever be eliminated. I'd like to have all experiments stopped, but at least if they're done in the right way with no abuse, I guess we'll have to go along with it. I can't bear to see anything or anyone suffer. There's an awful lot of needless experimentation. You need somebody to keep an eye on it all the time. To have innocents suffer is unthinkable. Most people don't even know what's going on. I have to do something about it in my lifetime.'

It was a tough job she had taken on. The conversation we had was constantly interrupted by a ringing telephone, telling her of some animal or other in distress. Newspapers reported that she had fourteen dogs of her own. 'I can't tell you how many I have got,' she told me. 'The reason I've got so many is that I'm always bringing them home.'

But some were plainly favourites – like Wesley Winfield, a shih tzu, and Buster Brown, one whose breed was less well established.

It was all a terribly personal thing. I asked her what happened when a beloved pet died. 'I can't talk about that,' she told me. 'I can't even look at their pictures.'

So she did everything she could to get the message across. As the year 2000 dawned, there was a web site for the League, now based in Washington and intended simply to lobby legislators.

It organized a 'National Spay Day'. It protested – by 'Special Alert' – against the US Army Air Force and Marines holding 'survival skills' training courses on which they were told to 'kill docile rabbits, chickens and goats as part of emergency food procurement exercises' and made representations to the Defense Department.

But then there was an agreement with the White House to incorporate non-animal experimentation in the Environmental Protection Agency's chemical testing programme.

The League supported President Bill Clinton's signing into law a bill against 'crush' videos – a fad in which women step on and kill a variety of small animals – which had come out into the open instead of being just part of an underground cult.

She had help from Terry in this. And she helped him, too – to record his own album.

But then she also had another man help her – Barry Comden, a restaurant host, twelve years her junior, whom she married in 1976. Their marriage was going to be unlike any of her others. They moved from Hollywood to the upper-class township of Santa Barbara. She wouldn't talk about him. She was now a private person and that was going to be the way she kept her private life and her private marriage. On the whole, she succeeded. *Who's Who* and most other reference works didn't even mention him. But the marriage didn't work any better than the others. They divorced in 1980. All she would say about it was, 'It's just better that we live apart.'

Years later, Comden would say that she kicked him out of her bed because she preferred to sleep with a dog. He was forced to take refuge in the guest house. 'She wanted the space in the main house to house some extra dogs.'

As he said: 'There was always a dog between us. She treated them better than me.' But he co-operated for a time. He said he got fed up with doing the cooking at home 'because she was too busy concocting gourmet treats for her fourteen pet pooches'. (The pets had their own kitchen.)

Comden's mother, Natalie Shapiro, was quoted as saying: 'Barry wouldn't be divorcing her but for those damned dogs. Doris loves the animals to the exclusion of everything else, including my son.'

Doris didn't attend the divorce court. She said that she and her fourth husband had been incompatible with each other and that was it. She was too busy building a series of air-conditioned kennels.

But A. E. Hotchner, who wrote her autobiography, *My Story*, (which Doris had been persuaded to publish by her close friend Jacqueline 'Valley of the Dolls' Susann), explained for her: 'She took Comden in like she takes in stray animals, but he broke her heart. She believed in him and when he took to his heels, she felt betrayed. I'm surprised the marriage lasted that long. It was a tragic affair. She's had some rotten blows in her life. She's been like one of those dolls that are filled up with air. When you push it down, it bounces back up. The sad thing is that when the doll gets old enough, it gets pushed down that one last time and it doesn't come up again.'

That was the reason, it was said, that she had become a recluse. But had she? Doris would always say that she wasn't that at all. She just had more important things to worry about.

The 'secrecy' of her marriage provided plenty of ammunition for the journalists and others who spread the rumours of what they said was her strange new lifestyle. One paper said she had become a bag lady – and she sued for libel. She asked $16 million. The *Globe* alleged that she 'rummages through trash cans looking for food scraps to make stew for her dogs'. That was about as far from the real Doris Day as you could get. Besides which, her dogs, the best-fed mutts in the world, were never served scraps.

Other stories were slightly less damaging, but didn't say the sort of nice things that had previously gone hand in hand with any references to either the virginal Doris or the sexy older woman in those figure-hugging suits. They said she was a hypochondriac who was constantly popping vitamins into her system. They said she was so scared of getting cancer that she lived in terror every day of her life. Her life, they suggested, was surrounded by her pets (which was partly true) and playing her own records (which was not). Why, the fans asked, didn't she go back to what they considered to be her real work. She was sorry that she didn't, but the bus had been missed. 'I love to work, but . . . *que sera sera,*' (which was probably not intended as a plug for any residual copies of her records that might be around).

They wrote nice letters about her clothes and she replied to say how much she enjoyed wearing them – except for the furs, which she now wishes she had never gone near. 'When I look back, I could die that I wore furs. It just breaks my heart that those films are playing and I just want everybody out there to know – all my friends – that I do not wear furs. I won't even sell them. I won't auction them. They're in cold storage and that's where they're gonna stay.'

Those friends always believed what she told them, although even as the years wore on, they didn't accept that she could really be called Doris. The very close ones called her Clara – because they thought she looked like a Clara.

If there was one human condition for which she felt concern equal to her feelings for animals, then it had to be AIDS. How indeed could she feel anything else after all those enjoyable movie associations with Rock Hudson?

In 1985, Hudson took part in a press conference to launch her new TV series. She was immensely shocked by the appearance of the man she had hardly seen since they last worked together. They kissed and cuddled before the cameras. She asked him if he had

Performing in 1977, the year after her fourth marriage
to restaurant host Barry Comden

met her grandson yet (Terry had married and had a son five years before). He said he had flu. She believed him.

It was to be his last public appearance. The next day he went into hospital with what was described as a 'possible heart attack'. He never came out of the hospital.

She complained to Hudson's publicist about subjecting him to the ordeal. But of Rock himself all she would say was: 'I never asked about his personal life. I didn't know and I wasn't part of it. And even if I did know details, I wouldn't dream of discussing it. He was a dear man and I loved him.' As she said: 'All my memories of working with him are of us just laughing and laughing. He had many friends, but I was one of the luckiest ones – I got to work with him.'

For a time she seemed to beat the system and went back to work, with a new TV series, *Doris Day's Best Friends*. It ran during the 1985–6 season on cable television's Christian Broadcast Network. The best friends all had four legs. But even she discovered there were not enough dogs to keep a TV series going. Then, in 1991, ABC announced that she would star in a collection of telefilms, playing a variety of characters, but it never happened.

What Doris Day enthusiasts might have wished for could not possibly be. A woman in her sixties and then seventies couldn't still play the sort of parts the fans had loved so much. And any records she might make couldn't possibly be like the ones that had gained such a following in the past. Maybe that was the problem. Her philosophy had always been: 'I honestly believed every word of what I sang or spoke and people respond to that.'

But were people ready to respond any more? There was another unspoken problem. Her real fans were being identified as gay men – and that could have been dangerous for her older, fading core audience. Nevertheless, this was a woman who had made thirty-nine films in the best part of twenty years, and in those years had achieved a following that was the envy of her contemporaries. She couldn't expect those to be forgotten. She wouldn't have wanted them to be either – and, I suspect, not merely for the money that the reruns on television still bring her.

She said she was happy just staying at home in Carmel doing the housework – 'I have the most wonderful collection of brooms.' But the memory of what Marty Melcher forced her to do would never go away and her home was a refuge from those memories. 'Why should I leave this darling place, where I'm so happy, to do something I didn't like?'

And, she protested, she was busy. 'I'm leading a constructive, conservative life. I work harder now than I ever did in the movies.' That was why she turned down a role in the *Hotel* series. She was also careful to deny that she was ever offered a part in either *Dynasty* or *Dallas*. She, competing with Joan Collins and Linda Evans? Part of Miss Ellie's family? Neither bears thinking about. (Mind you, she didn't specifically say she would have turned them down had they been offered, but you got the general idea.)

For years, she would deny that she had actually retired. To prove it, there were just occasional appearances on chat shows and TV specials, but it was always clear that she wasn't going back to work. It was, however, she said, just 'an extended vacation'. If so, she has given no indication of the holiday coming to an end. But then it had to be a holiday from her image as much as from her work.

When in December 1980, the National Film Theatre in London put on their major retrospective of Doris's films, they called it 'Move Over Misconceptions'. With that one title, they probably did her more favours than she could have appreciated.

The body of Doris Day's work was immensely varied and that is one of the things about her that is most missed. A fact that was underlined when the Foreign Press Association in California gave her their Lifetime Achievement Award.

The organizers of that had more luck than the Academy of Motion Picture Arts and Sciences. In 1988, they had her lined up for an extremely rare appearance – at that year's Oscar ceremony. As the producer Allan Carr said: 'We got a sitter for the dogs and she said yes.' But she didn't come. She tripped over a water sprinkler just before leaving Carmel and cancelled.

The request to her came a year after she had been asked to accept the Hommage acclaim at that year's Cannes Film Festival. For that, she had told the organizers she would think about it, and instructed them to 'call me next month'. Every month they did and every month she said the same thing. Just before the ceremony she told them no, she was too busy with the animals. 'Two of my dogs are having litters.'

'That is class,' said the *Today* newspaper in London. Others might have called it bad manners.

But people still wanted her. To underline that, script offers tumbled into her mail box almost as often as the distress calls on her telephone. But the vacation had given no signs of ending yet.

One reason could be that after she sang at private functions – which she still did and did well – she would be hoarse for months. If a doctor had dared to say that it all came from being around the animals, she would probably have walked out of his office and changed her medical practitioner.

She liked to seem modern and understanding. You couldn't condemn kids for taking drugs, she would say, because there were plenty of adults who did it, too – and how do you blame all adults? Besides, she remembered only too well the drug taking in her band-singing days (not that she took part in it, you understand).

'I don't look askance at modern youth. I love them. I think we should stop as adults in judging them and everyone. We should stop judging our young people too quickly and stop pointing the finger because that's not brother love, either. It really isn't.'

One could wish that her private life had been happier, that you didn't always feel that her work for animals was a way of sublimating her frustrations for personal contentment. But there were the odd moments to give her that happiness. Terry recovered from his own horrendous problems and went back to produce more records. If only, thought his mother's fans, he could have produced a new hit for his mother.

People wondered how she could just leave behind such a marvellous career. But that wasn't the way she saw it. 'When I first started out, I wasn't looking for a career. And I don't think of it as a career now. There is no such thing as a career man. So why should there be a career woman?'

Nevertheless, whatever it was you wanted to call it, it was over.

But there were frequent compensations. In 1993, now sixty-nine, she heard crowds humming and whistling the hits from *Calamity Jane*. Her home town of Carmel put on a $50-a-ticket event in her honour – including the showing of the film – in aid of a crime-busting scheme for the town. Carmel's former mayor, Clint Eastwood, told the guests: 'When I was a struggling contract player back in the 1950s, one of the things I had to do was take dance lessons. One day, they told me I'd be dancing with someone special. That special someone turned out to be Doris and it turned out to be the highlight of my career.' Doris Day was still a big enough name for the people at the event to pretend that they believed that conclusion.

And the following year, her hit from thirty years before, 'Perhaps, Perhaps, Perhaps', got into the charts once again when it was played on the soundtrack of the Australian film, *Strictly Ballroom*.

Tantalizingly, 'Perhaps, Perhaps, Perhaps' always seemed to sum up her reaction to that perpetual question about her future and the chance in a million that she might go back to work. Yet if she ever did end that retirement, it would have to be at the cost of the image that would haunt her for ever. As she once said: 'I don't even like apple pie. I prefer peach.'

But she would always surprise – and be surprised herself. Which was precisely what you might expect from a girl whose theme song was '*Que Sera Sera*'.